"Simple. Practical. Helpful. In *Habits of Grace*, Mathis writes brilliantly about three core spiritual disciplines that will help us realign our lives and strengthen our faith. In a world where everything seems to be getting more complicated, this book will help us to downshift and refocus on the things that matter most."

Louie Giglio, Pastor, Passion City Church, Atlanta; Founder,
Passion Conferences

"Although this little book says what many others say about Bible reading, prayer, and Christian fellowship (with two or three others tacked on), its great strength and beauty is that it nurtures my resolve to read the Bible and it makes me hungry to pray. If the so-called 'means of grace' are laid out as nothing more than duties, the hinge of sanctification is obligation. But in this case, the means of grace are rightly perceived as gracious gifts and signs that God is at work in us, which increases our joy as we stand on the cusp of Christian freedom under the glories of King Jesus."

D. A. Carson, Research Professor of New Testament,
Trinity Evangelical Divinity School; cofounder, The Gospel Coalition

"Most people assume that disciplined training is necessary for attaining any skill—professional, academic, or athletic. But for some reason, Christians do not see this principle applying to their Christian lives. In his excellent book, *Habits of Grace*, David Mathis makes a compelling case for the importance of the spiritual disciplines, and he does so in such a winsome way that will motivate all of us to practice the spiritual disciplines of the Christian life. This book will be great both for new believers just starting on their journey and as a refresher course for those of us already along the way."

Jerry Bridges, author, *The Pursuit of Holiness*

"David Mathis has more than accomplished his goal of writing an introduction to the spiritual disciplines. What I love most about the book is how Mathis presents the disciplines—or 'means of grace' as he prefers to describe them—as habits to be cultivated in order to enjoy Jesus. The biblical practices Mathis explains are not ends—that was the mistake of the Pharisees in Jesus's day and of legalists in our time. Rather they are means by which we seek, savor, and enjoy Jesus Christ. May the Lord use this book to help you place yourself 'in the way of allurement' that results in an increase of your joy in Jesus."

Donald S. Whitney, Associate Professor of Biblical Spirituality,
Senior Associate Dean of the School of Theology, The Southern
Baptist Theological Seminary; author, *Spiritual Disciplines for the
Christian Life*

"So often as we consider the spiritual disciplines, we think of what we must do individually. Mathis takes a different approach that is both insightful and refreshing. Along with our personal time of prayer and reading, we are encouraged to seek advice from seasoned saints, have conversations about Bible study with others, and pray together. The Christian life, including the disciplines, isn't meant to be done in isolation. Mathis's depth of biblical knowledge along with his practical guidance and gracious delivery will leave you eager to pursue the disciplines, shored up by the grace of God."

Trillia Newbell, author, *United: Captured by God's Vision for Diversity* and *Fear and Faith*

"This is the kind of book I turn to periodically to help examine and recalibrate my heart, my priorities, and my walk with the Lord. David Mathis has given us a primer for experiencing and exuding ever-growing delight in Christ through grace-initiated intentional habits that facilitate the flow of yet fuller springs of grace into and through our lives."

Nancy DeMoss Wolgemuth, author; radio host, *Revive Our Hearts*

"There is not a Christian in the world who has mastered the spiritual disciplines. In fact, the more we grow in grace, the more we realize how little we know of hearing from God, speaking to God, and meditating on God. Our maturity reveals our inadequacy. *Habits of Grace* is a powerful guide to the spiritual disciplines. It offers basic instructions to new believers while bringing fresh encouragement to those who have walked with the Lord for many years. It is a joy to commend it to you."

Tim Challies, author, *The Next Story*; blogger, *Challies.com*

"When I was growing up, spiritual disciplines were often surrounded by an air of legalism. But today the pendulum has swung in the other direction: it seems that family and private devotions have fallen off the radar. The very word *habits* can be a turnoff, especially in a culture of distraction and autonomy. Yet character is largely a bundle of habits. Christ promises to bless us through his means of grace: his Word preached and written, baptism, and the Lord's Supper. Like a baby's first cry, prayer is the beginning of that life of response to grace given, and we never grow out of it. Besides prayer, there are other habits that grace motivates and shapes. I'm grateful for *Habits of Grace* bringing the disciplines back into the conversation and, hopefully, back into our practice as well."

Michael Horton, J. Gresham Machen Professor of Systematic Theology and Apologetics, Westminster Seminary California; author, *Calvin on the Christian Life*

"David Mathis has given us a book on the spiritual disciplines that is practical, actionable, and accessible. He speaks with a voice that neither scolds nor overwhelms, offering encouragement through suggestions and insights to help even the newest believer find a rhythm by which to employ these means of grace. A treatment of the topic that is wonderfully uncomplicated and thorough, *Habits of Grace* offers both a place to start for beginners and a path to grow for those seasoned in the faith."

Jen Wilkin, author, *Women of the Word*; Bible study teacher

"I am drawn to books that I know are first lived out in the messiness of life before finding their way onto clean sheets of paper. This is one of those books! David has found a well-worn path to Jesus through the habits of grace he commends to us. I am extremely grateful for David's commitment to take the timeless message in this book and communicate it in language that is winsome to the mind and warm to the heart. This book has the breadth of a literature review that reads like a devotional. I am eager to get it into the hands of our campus ministry staff and see it being read in dorm rooms and student centers across the country."

Matt Bradner, Regional Director, Campus Outreach

"David Mathis has provided us with a gospel-driven, Word-centered, Christ-exalting vision of Christian spiritual practices. Furthermore, he understands that sanctification is a community project: the local church rightly looms large in *Habits of Grace*. This book is perfect for small group study, devotional reading, or for passing on to a friend who is thinking about this topic for the first time. I give it my highest recommendation."

Nathan A. Finn, Dean, The School of Theology and Missions, Union University

Habits of Grace

Enjoying Jesus through the
Spiritual Disciplines

David Mathis

Foreword by John Piper

CROSSWAY®

WHEATON, ILLINOIS

Habits of Grace: Enjoying Jesus through the Spiritual Disciplines

Copyright © 2016 by David C. Mathis

Published by Crossway
       1300 Crescent Street
       Wheaton, Illinois 60187

Cover design: Jeff Miller, Faceout Studio

Cover image: Benjamin Devine

First printing 2016

Printed in the United States of America

Trade paperback ISBN: 978-1-4335-5047-8
ePub ISBN: 978-1-4335-5050-8
PDF ISBN: 978-1-4335-5048-5
Mobipocket ISBN: 978-1-4335-5049-2

Library of Congress Cataloging-in-Publication Data
Mathis, David, 1980–
   Habits of grace : enjoying Jesus through the spiritual
disciplines / David Mathis ; foreword by John Piper.
     pages cm
   Includes bibliographical references and index.
   ISBN 978-1-4335-5047-8 (tp)
   1. Spiritual life—Christianity. 2. Christian life. I. Title.
BV4501.3.M284   2016
248.4'6—dc23   2015023865

Crossway is a publishing ministry of Good News Publishers.

LB   27 26 25 24 23 22 21 20 19 18 17
16 15 14 13 12 11 10 9 8 7 6 5 4

To Carson and Coleman
May he give you a palate
for the ancient recipes

Contents

Foreword

by John Piper

―――――――

I don't even think David intended this, but his title and sub-title are a chiasm. And I like it so much, I'm going to build my foreword around it. A chiasm (taken from the Greek letter *chi*, which looks like an X) is a sequence of thoughts in which the first and last member correspond, and the second and second-to-last member correspond, and so on, with a hinge thought in the middle. So the title of the book looks like this in a chiasm:

> *Habits*
>   *of Grace:*
>   *Enjoying Jesus*
>   *through the Spiritual*
> *Disciplines*

Habits corresponds to *Disciplines*. *Grace* corresponds to *Spiritual*. And *Enjoying Jesus* is the hinge. This is loaded with implications for why David's book is worth reading.

The chiasm, and the book, and the theology behind it demand that *enjoying Jesus* be the hinge. But "hinge" only signifies the swing position in the middle of the other thoughts. There is always more to it than that. In this case, the hinge is the goal of all the rest.

David is writing a book to help you enjoy Jesus. In doing that, he is not trying to be nice. He's trying to be nuclear. His way of thinking about enjoying Jesus is explosive. If you enjoy Jesus more than life (Matt. 10:38), you will live with a radical abandon for Jesus that will make the world wonder. Enjoyment of Jesus is not like icing on the cake; it's like powder in the shell.

Not only is enjoying Jesus explosively transforming in the way we live; it is also essential for making Jesus look great. And that is why we have the Holy Spirit. Jesus said the Spirit came to glorify him (John 16:14). The primary mission of the Spirit—and his people—is to show that Jesus is more glorious than anyone or anything else. It cannot be done by those who find this world more enjoyable than Jesus. They make the world look great. Therefore, the ultimate aim of the Christian life—and the universe—hangs on the people of God enjoying the Son of God.

But this is beyond us. Our hearts default to enjoying the world more than Jesus. This is why the hinge thought—enjoying Jesus—is bracketed on both sides by *grace* and *spiritual*.

> *Grace*
> > *Enjoying Jesus*
> *Spiritual*

Grace is the free and sovereign work of God to do for us what we cannot do for ourselves, even though we don't deserve it. *Spiritual* is the biblical word to describe what has been brought about by the Holy Spirit. "Spiritual" does not mean religious, or mystical, or new-age-like. It means: caused and shaped by God's Spirit.

So the point is this: God almighty, by his grace and by his Spirit, does not leave us to ourselves when it comes to enjoying Jesus. He helps us. He does not say, "Delight yourself in the LORD" (Ps. 37:4), and then merely stand back and watch to see if we can. He makes a covenant with us and says, "I will put my Spirit within you, and cause you to walk in my statutes" (Ezek. 36:27). He causes what he commands. Enjoying Jesus is not optional. It is a duty. But it is also a gift—spiritual and gracious.

But the gift comes through means. This is why *Grace* is flanked by *Habits*, and *Spiritual* is flanked by *Disciplines*.

> *Habits*
> > *of Grace:*
> > > *Enjoying Jesus*
> > > *through the Spiritual*
> *Disciplines*

The Bible does not say, "God is at work in you to bring about his good purposes, *therefore* stay in bed." It says, "Work out your salvation, *because* God is at work in you" (see Phil. 2:12–13). God's work does not make our work unnecessary; it makes it possible. "I worked harder than any of them, though it was not I, but the grace of God that is with me" (1 Cor. 15:10). Grace does not just pardon our failures; it empowers our successes—like successfully enjoying Jesus more than life.

This book is about grace-empowered *habits*, and Spirit-empowered *disciplines*. These are the means God has given for drinking at the fountain of life. They don't earn the enjoyment. They receive it. They are not payments for pleasure; they are pipelines. The psalmist does not say, "You *sell* them drink," but, "You *give* them drink from the river of your delights" (Ps. 36:8). But all of us leak. We all need inspiration and instruction for how to drink—again and again. Habitually.

If you have never read a book on "habits of grace" or "spiritual disciplines," start with this one. If you are a veteran lover of the river of God, but, for some reason, have recently been wandering aimlessly in the desert, this book will be a good way back.

John Piper
desiringGod.org
Minneapolis, Minnesota

Preface

I make no pretense that this is the definitive book, or anything close to it, on the spiritual disciplines—better, "the means of grace." In fact, I've been intentional to keep things relatively brief. Think of this as an introduction or orientation. Many important lessons are left to others to provide in more extended treatments.[1] In particular, I am eager to help Christians young and old simplify their approach to their various personal habits of grace, or spiritual disciplines, by highlighting the three key principles of ongoing grace: hearing God's voice (his word), having his ear (prayer), and belonging to his body (fellowship).

This simplified approach, and many of the ideas developed in the pages ahead, were forged first in the classroom at Bethlehem College & Seminary, where I've taught "the disciplines" to the third-year collegiates. Next I made the effort to get the concepts the students seemed to find most helpful into article form at desiringGod.org. The response was encouraging, and Crossway was kind enough to provide the opportunity to bring the thoughts together and extend them in this form.

This volume is intentionally half the size of most others on

---

[1] In particular, as you'll find throughout the book, I am indebted to three texts I highly recommend—two old friends and one new: Donald S. Whitney, *Spiritual Disciplines for the Christian Life*, rev. ed. (Colorado Springs: NavPress, 2014); John Piper, *When I Don't Desire God: How to Fight for Joy* (Wheaton, IL: Crossway, 2004); and Timothy Keller, *Prayer: Experiencing Awe and Intimacy with God* (New York: Dutton, 2014).

the disciplines. I hope that some readers will go from here to the larger books. But I wanted to provide something shorter, yet still cover the major topics, in hopes of making a simplified approach to the means of grace accessible to others who wouldn't take up the bigger volumes.

However, the roots of this book go back long before teaching college and writing articles. Seeds were sown earlier than I can even remember by my parents and childhood church in Spartanburg, South Carolina. Every morning Pop was up early reading his Bible and praying before heading into the dental office, and Mom typically had her Bible open on the dining room table as she dipped into the Book during the day. I frequently heard refreshers on the basics in varying detail and depth in elementary, middle, and high school classes at church.

In college, through the ministry of Campus Outreach, I was discipled during the semester and shaped by summer training projects. When I was a college junior, a discipler introduced me to Donald S. Whitney's *Spiritual Disciplines for the Christian Life*. I began teaching "how to have a quiet time" to younger students in the context of life-on-life discipleship, and then continued doing so on staff with Campus Outreach in Minneapolis. These experiences eventually led to instructing college juniors at Bethlehem.

I must mention the incalculable influence of John Piper, with whom I have worked closely since 2006. For those who know his ministry of preaching and writing, John's fingerprints will be unmistakable in these pages, both in explicit quotations and in structures of thought and instincts I can't shake, and wouldn't want to. His 2004 book *When I Don't Desire God* is the place to find his most concentrated practical teaching on Bible intake and prayer, but gold nuggets on the means of grace, and his own habits, are scattered throughout his corpus, especially in his annual new-year sermons on Bible and prayer available at desiringGod.org, and his answers to the litany of practical questions that come through the *Ask Pastor John* daily podcast.

Just after receiving the invitation to publish this book, I read Timothy Keller's *Prayer: Experiencing Awe and Intimacy with God*. You will see in part 2, on prayer, that already I'm gleaning much from Keller's insights, and I greatly commend his book. My hope is that the little bit I have to say about prayer will point you in the right direction, and then sooner, rather than later, you will take it to the next level, and more, with Keller's remarkable guide.

How This Book Is Different

I eagerly send you to the longer texts on the disciplines, but that doesn't mean I've written this book merely as a summary, with nothing distinct to contribute. Perhaps the key distinguishing feature of this book, in addition to its brevity, is the threefold organizational scheme we've already noted. Here we cast the disciplines not as ten or twelve (or more) distinct practices to work into your life, but as three key principles (God's voice, God's ear, and God's people), which then are fleshed out in countless creative and helpful habits in the varying lives of believers in their differing contexts.

In particular, this structure restores fellowship as a means of grace to its essential place in the Christian life. Piper's, Keller's, and Whitney's books focus on personal disciplines, and include no extended sections, much less a full chapter, on the role of fellowship.[2] In structuring this book in three parts, similar practices can be grouped and understood together, such that individual chapters are shorter and designed for reading in one sitting. My hope is that this will help you move toward application in your own practices by making clear that the point isn't

---

[2] Whitney has made a good effort to compensate for it with *Spiritual Disciplines within the Church: Participating Fully in the Body of Christ* (Chicago: Moody, 1996).

to practice at all times in one's Christian walk every single specific discipline addressed, but to understand the key pathways of ongoing grace and seek to create regular habits for these principles in life.

At Crossway's request, I've written a study guide to accompany this book for those who would like to deepen their reflections and applications. It is designed for both individual and group study, and is available in workbook format.

My prayer is that you will not come away exasperated that you simply don't have time to put into practice all that this book commends. Rather, in its very structure, the book aims to help you see how realistic and life-giving it can be to integrate God's means of grace into daily habits of life.

And alongside the emphasis on fellowship, this book also hopes to make the pursuit of joy more central, explicit, and pronounced than has typically been the case in many texts on the disciplines.

My Dream and Prayer for You

My prayer for you as you read is that you would find the means of grace to be practical, realistic, and desirable in your pursuit of joy in Christ. I hope that there are many things here beneficial to a general Christian audience, but that there will be a special appeal to college students and young adults who are learning to fly for themselves for the first time in the various rhythms and practices of the Christian life.

My dream is that this book would serve you with simplicity, stability, confidence, power, and joy. *Simplicity* in that looking at the means of grace in three main channels will help you understand the matrix of grace for living the Christian life and create practical pathways (your own habits) that are realistic and life-giving in your unique season of life. *Stability* in that getting to know your own soul, and creating rhythms and practices, will help you weather the ups and downs of life in this fallen world with the contentment that comes, in some measure, from knowing ourselves and learning ways in which we can help "lift your drooping hands and strengthen your weak knees, and make straight paths for your feet" (Heb. 12:12–13) and "keep yourselves in the love of God" (Jude 21). *Confidence* in that as you walk these paths, you'll see how God is faithful to sustain us and give us "grace to help in time of need" (Heb. 4:16). *Power* in that hearing his word, having his ear, and belonging to his body fill our souls with spiritual energy and strength for the pouring out of ourselves in ministry and mission. And *joy* to satisfy our deepest longings that will only be met in their fullness when we see the God-man face to face and live in perfect communion with him, and all our fellows in him, forever.

The note we will strike again and again, without any apology, is that the means of grace, fleshed out in our various habits of grace, are to be for us *means of joy* in God, and thus means of his glory. And so the simplicity, stability, confidence, power, and joy of God himself stand behind these means. These are the paths of his promise. He stands ready to pour out his wonderfully wild and lavish grace through these channels. Are you ready?

Introduction

Grace Gone Wild

———

The grace of God is on the loose. Contrary to our expectations, counter to our assumptions, frustrating our judicial sentiments, and mocking our craving for control, the grace of God is turning the world upside down. God is shamelessly pouring out his lavish favor on undeserving sinners of all stripes and thoroughly stripping away our self-sufficiency.

Before turning our focus to "the means of grace," and the practices ("habits") that ready us to go on receiving God's grace in our lives, this much must be clear from the outset: The grace of God is gloriously beyond our skill and technique. The means of grace are not about earning God's favor, twisting his arm, or controlling his blessing, but readying ourselves for consistent saturation in the roll of his tides.

Grace has been on the move since before creation, roaming wild and free. Even before the foundation of the world, it was the untamed grace of God that jumped the bounds of time and space and considered a yet-to-be-created people in connection with his Son, and chose us in him (Eph. 1:4). It was in love—to the praise of his glorious grace—that "he predestined us for adoption as sons through Jesus" (Eph. 1:5). Such divine choice was not based on foreseeing anything good in us. He chose us by grace—not "on the basis of works; otherwise grace would no longer be grace" (Rom. 11:5–6). It was "not because of our works but because of his own purpose and grace, which he gave us in Christ Jesus before the ages began" (2 Tim. 1:9).

With patience, then—through creation, fall, and flood, through Adam, Noah, Abraham, and King David—God prepared the way. Humanity waited and groaned, gathering up the crumbs of his compassion as a foretaste of some feast to come. The prophets "prophesied about the grace that was to be yours" (1 Pet. 1:10). And in the fullness of time, it came. He came.

Invading Our Space

Now "the grace of God has appeared" (Titus 2:11). Grace couldn't be kept from becoming flesh and dwelling among us in the God-man, full of grace and truth (John 1:14). From his fullness we have all received grace upon grace (John 1:16). The law was given through Moses, but grace and truth are here in him (John 1:17). Grace has a face.

But grace would not be restricted even here, even in this man. Grace would not just be embodied but break the chains to roam the globe unfettered. It was sheer grace that united us by faith to Jesus, Grace Incarnate, and blessed us in him "with every spiritual blessing in the heavenly places" (Eph. 1:3). In grace were we called with effect (Gal. 1:6) and given new birth in our souls. Because of grace unmeasured, boundless, free, now our once-dead hearts beat and our once-lifeless lungs breathe. Only through grace do we believe (Acts 18:27) and only in grace do we receive "repentance leading to a knowledge of the truth" (2 Tim. 2:25).

But such wild grace keeps going. We are given the Spirit of grace, experience our long-planned adoption, and enabled to cry, "Abba! Father!" (Rom. 8:15). We receive "the forgiveness of our trespasses, according to the riches of his grace" (Eph. 1:7).

Grace keeps breaking through barriers and casting away restraints. *Grace justifies.* A perfect, unimpeachable, divinely approved, humanly applied righteousness is ours in this union with Jesus. We are "justified by his grace as a gift" (Rom. 3:24; Titus 3:7). Through this one man Jesus, we are counted among "those who receive the abundance of grace and the free gift of righteousness" (Rom. 5:17). And so we happily say with Paul, "I do not nullify the grace of God, for if righteousness were through the law, then Christ died for no purpose" (Gal. 2:21).[1]

Breaking into Our Lives

And just when we think we have been carried far enough, that God has done for us all that we could imagine and more, grace shatters the mold again. *Grace sanctifies.* It is too wild to let us stay in love with unrighteousness. Too free to leave us in slavery to sin. Too untamed to let our lusts go unconquered. Grace's power is too uninhibited to not unleash us for the happiness of true holiness.

So it is that we "grow in the grace and knowledge of our Lord and Savior Jesus Christ" (2 Pet. 3:18) and live "not under law but under grace" (Rom. 6:14). Grace abounds not through our continuing in sin, but through our Spirit-empowered, ongoing liberation (Rom. 6:1). Grace is too strong to leave us passive, too potent to let us wallow in the mire of our sins and weaknesses. "My grace is sufficient for you," Jesus says, "for my power is made perfect in weakness" (2 Cor. 12:9). It is the grace of God that gives us his "means of grace" for our ongoing perseverance

---

[1] For more on justification by faith alone, and in particular how it relates to sanctification and the Christian's pursuit of growth and holiness in the Christian life, see "The Search for Sanctification's Holy Grail," in *Acting the Miracle: God's Work and Ours in the Mystery of Sanctification*, ed. John Piper and David Mathis (Wheaton, IL: Crossway, 2013), 13–27.

and growth and joy this side of the coming new creation. And the grace of God inspires and empowers the various habits and practices by which we avail ourselves of God's means.

Flooding the Future

Just when we're sure it is done, and certain that some order must be restored and some boundary established, God's grace not only floods our future in this life but also spans the divide into the next, and pours out onto the plains of our eternity. *Grace glorifies.*

If the Scriptures didn't make plain this story of our glory, we'd be scared to even dream of such grace. Not only will Jesus be glorified in us, but we will be glorified in him, "according to the grace of our God and the Lord Jesus Christ" (2 Thess. 1:12). He is "the God of all grace, who has called you to his eternal glory in Christ" (1 Pet. 5:10). So Peter tells us to "set your hope fully on the grace that will be brought to you at the revelation of Jesus Christ" (1 Pet. 1:13). It will be indescribably stunning in the coming ages as he shows "the immeasurable riches of his grace in kindness toward us in Christ Jesus" (Eph. 2:7). Even the most mature among us have only begun to taste the grace of God.

Chosen before time. Called with effect. United to Jesus in faith and repentance. Adopted and forgiven. Justified. Sanctified. Glorified. And satisfied forever. This is grace gone wonderfully wild. This is the flood of God's favor in which we discover the power and practice of the means of grace.

Put Yourself in the Path of God's Grace

It is in this endless sea of his grace that we walk the path of the Christian life and take steps of grace-empowered effort and initiative. It works something like this.

I can flip a switch, but I don't provide the electricity. I can turn on a faucet, but I don't make the water flow. There will be no light and no liquid refreshment without someone else providing it. And so it is for the Christian with the ongoing grace of God. His grace is essential for our spiritual lives, but we don't control the supply. We can't make the favor of God flow, but he has given us circuits to connect and pipes to open expectantly. There are paths along which he has promised his favor.

As we have celebrated above, our God is lavish in his grace; he is free to liberally dispense his goodness without even the least bit of cooperation and preparation on our part, and often he does. But he also has his regular channels. And we can routinely avail ourselves of these revealed paths of blessing—or neglect them to our detriment.

Where the Grace Keeps Passing

"The essence of the Christian life," writes John Piper, "is learning to fight for joy in a way that does not replace grace." We cannot earn God's grace or make it flow apart from his free gift. But we can position ourselves to go on getting as he keeps on giving. We can "fight to walk in the paths where he has promised his blessings."[2] We can ready ourselves to remain receivers along his regular routes, sometimes called "the spiritual disciplines," or even better, "the means of grace."[3]

Such practices need not be fancy or highfalutin.[4] They are the

---

[2] John Piper, *When I Don't Desire God: How to Fight for Joy* (Wheaton, IL: Crossway, 2004), 43–44.

[3] I prefer "means of grace" to "spiritual disciplines." In one sense, this is a book essentially concerned with what many would call the Christian "spiritual disciplines." However, I find that the language of "means of grace" coheres more consistently with the theology of the Bible about such practices and helps to keep the key emphases in their proper places. "Means of grace," according to D. A. Carson, is "a lovely expression less susceptible to misinterpretation than spiritual disciplines." Carson, "Spiritual Disciplines," in *Themelios*, 36, no. 3 (November 2011).

[4] As we will see, the means of grace are first and foremost principles, which can be fleshed out in countless, creative practices ("habits").

stuff of everyday, basic Christianity—unimpressively mundane, but spectacularly potent by the Spirit. While there's no final and complete list of such practices, the long tally of helpful habits can be clustered underneath three main principles: hearing God's voice, having his ear, and belonging to his body. Or simply: word, prayer, and fellowship.[5]

In the last generation, we have seen some resurgence of interest among Christians in the spiritual disciplines, many of which were considered "means of grace" by our spiritual ancestors. "The doctrine of the disciplines," says J. I. Packer, "is really a restatement and extension of classical Protestant teaching on the means of grace."[6] Whatever the term, the key is that God has revealed certain channels through which he regularly pours out his favor. And we're foolish not to take his word on them and build habits of spiritual life around them.

What Means of Grace Means and Doesn't

To put *means* with *grace* might endanger the free nature of grace. But it need not do so—not if the means are coordinate with receiving and the exertions of effort are graciously supplied. This is emphatically the case for the Christian. Here there is no ground for boasting.[7]

---

[5] John Frame, in *Systematic Theology* (Phillipsburg, NJ: P&R, 2013), organizes the means of grace under these three headings. This way of categorizing it is close to Luke's summary of early-church life in Acts 2:42: "they devoted themselves to the apostles' teaching [the word] and the fellowship, to the breaking of bread [which we categorize under fellowship] and the prayers." J. C. Ryle shows a similar system of categorization when he writes, "The 'means of grace' are such as Bible reading, private prayer, and regularly worshiping God in Church, wherein one hears the Word taught and participates in the Lord's Supper. I lay it down as a simple matter of fact that no one who is careless about such things must ever expect to make much progress in sanctification. I can find no record of any eminent saint who ever neglected them. They are appointed channels through which the Holy Spirit conveys fresh supplies of grace to the soul and strengthens the work which He has begun in the inward man. . . . Our God is a God who works by means, and He will never bless the soul of that man who pretends to be so high and spiritual that he can get on without them." J. C. Ryle, *Holiness: Its Nature, Hindrances, Difficulties, and Roots* (Peabody, MN: Hendrickson, 2007), 26.

[6] Foreword for Donald S. Whitney, *Spiritual Disciplines for the Christian Life*, rev. ed. (Colorado Springs, CO: NavPress, 2014), ix–x.

[7] Along with the Reformed tradition of Christian theology, I mean something distinctly Protestant by "means of grace." I do not believe that the various "means of grace" function auto-

The one on whom we lean is "the God of all grace" (1 Pet. 5:10). He not only elects the undeserving without condition (Rom. 8:29–33; Eph. 1:4) and works in them the miracle of new birth and the gift of faith, but he also freely declares them righteous by that faith ("justification") and begins supplying the flow of spiritual life and energy to experience the joy of increasing Christlikeness.

As we have seen, God's immense flood of grace not only sees us as holy in Christ but also progressively produces holy desires in us ("sanctification"). It is grace to be forgiven of sinful acts, and grace to be supplied the heart for righteous ones. It is grace that we are increasingly "conformed to the image of his Son" (Rom. 8:29), and grace that he doesn't leave us in the misery of our sin but pledges to bring to completion the good work he has begun in us (Phil. 1:6).

For the glory of God, the good of others, and the satisfaction of our souls, the aim of the Christian life is our coming to share in such Christlikeness or godliness—which is "holiness" rightly understood. And all our exertions of effort toward that goal are gifts of grace.

Train Yourself for Godliness

Yes, it is grace, and yes, we expend effort. And so the apostle Paul says to his protégé, "Train yourself for godliness" (1 Tim. 4:7). Discipline yourself for growth. Take regular action to get more of God in your mind and your heart, and echo his ways

---

matically (*ex opere operato* in the Catholic tradition), but are God's promised paths of blessing when received with conscious, active faith in God as the giver through Jesus Christ. Grace, then, is dispensed not by the church, but by Jesus himself. As Scottish theologian James Bannerman writes, "It is not the Church that governs and dispenses ordinances and spiritual graces in his name, and by reason of his original gift and endowment to her, but Christ who, personally present, governs and administers ordinances and blessing through the Church. The Church has no store of life apart from Christ being in it; the ordinances of the Church have no deposit of grace apart from Christ present with them; the office-bearers of the Church have no gift or power, or authority, or action, apart from Christ ruling and acting by them." James Bannerman, *The Church of Christ*, vol. 1 (Vestavia Hills, AL: Solid Ground Christian Books, 2009), 199.

in your life—which will make you increasingly like him ("godliness"). It's a gift, and we receive it as we become it.

Paul's own reliance on God for ongoing grace is a powerful testimony to this Christian dynamic of the means of grace and the habits of life we cultivate. He says in 1 Corinthians 15:10, "By the grace of God I am what I am. . . . I worked harder than any of them, though it was not I, but the grace of God that is with me." God's grace didn't make Paul passive but supplied the energy for discipline and effort, and every ounce of energy expended was all of grace.

And Paul says in Romans 15:18, "I will not venture to speak of anything except what Christ has accomplished through me." Jesus's grace, in this instance, didn't mean accomplishing his purpose despite Paul, or apart from him, but *through* him. Where does the apostle get the power to labor and expend such spiritual effort? "I toil, struggling with all his energy that he powerfully works within me" (Col. 1:29).

How to Receive the Gift of Effort

This dynamic is true not just because Paul is an apostle, but because he is a Christian. So he says to every believer, "Work out your own salvation with fear and trembling," because of this great promise: "For it is God who works in you, both to will and to work for his good pleasure" (Phil. 2:12–13). And so the majestic epistle to the Hebrews closes with a prayer for God's "working in us that which is pleasing in his sight" (Heb. 13:20–21).

The way to receive the gift of God's empowering our actions is to do the actions. If he gives the gift of effort, we receive that gift *by* expending the effort. When he gives the grace of growing in holiness, we don't receive that gift apart from becoming more holy. When he gives us the desire to get more of him in the Scriptures, or in prayer, or among his people, we don't receive that gift without experiencing the desire and living out the pursuits that flow from it.

Lay Yourself in the Way of Allurement

Zacchaeus may have been a wee little man, but he modeled this big reality by positioning himself along the path of grace. He couldn't force Jesus's hand, he couldn't make grace flow automatically, but he could put himself by faith along the path where Grace was coming (Luke 19:1–10). The same was true of blind Bartimaeus (Luke 18:35–43). He couldn't earn the restoration of his sight, but he could station himself along the route of grace where Jesus might give the gift as he passed that way.

"Think of the Spiritual Disciplines," says Donald S. Whitney, "as ways we can place ourselves in the path of God's grace and seek him as Bartimaeus and Zacchaeus placed themselves in Jesus's path and sought him."[8] Or as Jonathan Edwards put it, you can "endeavor to promote spiritual appetites by *laying yourself in the way of allurement*."[9] We cannot force Jesus's hand, but we can put ourselves along the paths of grace where we can be expectant of his blessing.

God's regular channels of grace, as we will see, are his voice, his ear, and his body. He often showers his people with unexpected favor. But typically the grace that sends our roots deepest, truly grows us up in Christ, prepares our soul for a new day, produces lasting spiritual maturity, and increases the current of our joy streams are the ordinary and unspectacular paths of fellowship, prayer, and Bible intake given practical expression in countless forms and habits.

---

[8] Whitney, *Spiritual Disciplines*, 13.

[9] "The Spiritual Blessings of the Gospel Represented by a Feast," in *Sermons and Discourses, 1723–1729*, ed. Kenneth Minkema, vol. 14 of *The Works of Jonathan Edwards* (New Haven, CT: Yale University Press, 1997), 286. Emphasis added.

While these simple habits of grace may seem as unimpressive as everyday switches and faucets, through them God regularly stands ready to give his true light and the water of life.

The Great End of the Means

Before we begin to say more about Jesus's word, his ear, and his church in the pages ahead, we need to make clear what is the greatest grace along these paths: Jesus himself. The great end of the means is knowing and enjoying him. The final joy in any truly Christian discipline or practice or rhythm of life is, in the words of the apostle, "the surpassing worth of knowing Christ Jesus my Lord" (Phil. 3:8). "This is eternal life," and this is the goal of the means of grace: "that they know you the only true God, and Jesus Christ whom you have sent" (John 17:3).

When all is said and done, our hope is not to be a skilled Bible reader, practiced pray-er, and faithful churchman, but to be the one who "understands and knows me, that I am the LORD who practices steadfast love, justice, and righteousness in the earth" (Jer. 9:23–24). And so our heartbeat in the habits we develop for hearing every word, speaking every prayer, and participating in every act of fellowship is Hosea 6:3: "Let us know; let us press on to know the LORD." Knowing and enjoying Jesus is the final end of hearing his voice, having his ear, and belonging to his body.

The means of grace, and their many good expressions, will serve to make us more like him, but only as our focus returns continually to Christ himself, not our own Christlikeness. It is in "beholding the glory of the Lord" that we "are being transformed into the same image from one degree of glory to another" (2 Cor. 3:18). Spiritual growth is a marvelous effect of such practices, but in a sense it is only a side effect. The heart is knowing and enjoying Jesus.

The Means of Grace and the Things of Earth

One important question our study raises is how these means of grace relate to the rest of God's creation. In an important sense, all of God's creation can serve as means of his grace, not just his word, prayer, and fellowship.[10] My friend and fellow pastor Joe Rigney skillfully addresses this in *The Things of Earth: Treasuring God by Enjoying His Gifts*.[11] His chapter on "Rhythms of Godwardness" intersects most explicitly with our focus on the means of grace and their habits. He writes about "two different types of godwardness . . . direct godwardness and indirect godwardness."[12]

Rigney's focus is on the second type and how we can treasure the God of heaven in the things of earth, while this book addresses the first—treasuring God through his appointed means of grace, those special channels through which he supplies ongoing blessing to his church. This twofold model (direct and indirect godwardness) serves Rigney's project well, but our inclusion of fellowship, not just God's word and prayer, as a means of grace raises a cluster of questions: Is corporate Christianity to be considered direct or indirect godwardness? Is it direct when we're gathered for corporate worship and indirect when we're conversing with each other about gospel realities? Or even more specifically, is it direct when we're singing (to God) in corporate worship but indirect when we're listening to a preacher? Is sharing in the Lord's Supper direct or indirect? The twofold concept works well for personal Bible meditation and prayer on the one hand, and for vocation and recreation

---

[10] For one, his word is not only the "special revelation" of the Scriptures, but also the "general revelation" of the skies, and all creation. "The heavens declare the glory of God, and the sky above proclaims his handiwork. Day to day pours out speech, and night to night reveals knowledge" (Ps. 19:1–2).

[11] Joe Rigney, *The Things of Earth: Treasuring God by Enjoying His Gifts* (Wheaton, IL: Crossway, 2015). John Piper also gives a chapter to "How to Wield the World in the Fight for Joy," in *When I Don't Desire God*.

[12] Rigney, *Things of Earth*, 121.

on the other, but the clarity breaks down when we turn to corporate godwardness, which doesn't fit well as "direct" or "indirect."

One way forward, at least for this book, is to consider "corporate godwardness" its own category alongside the direct godwardness of personal Bible meditation and prayer and the indirect godwardness of engaging with the things of earth. Certainly communing intentionally with fellow Christians about the things of heaven is fundamentally different than interacting with nonbelievers about sports and the weather, or fellow believers for that matter. If we add a third category and make it a triad, then this book is taken up mainly with two: direct godwardness in parts 1 and 2 and corporate godwardness in part 3.[13]

Your Habits, God's Grace

The means of grace are God's promised channels of continuing grace, received by faith. Infinite grace is behind us, and infinite grace lies ahead, and through his appointed means of grace, God is pleased to supply ongoing life and energy and health and strength to our souls. The means of grace fill our tank for the pursuit of joy, for the good of others, and for the glory of God. They are *spiritual* blessings, not the gravely mistimed *material* blessings promised prematurely in the so-called "prosperity gospel." And they are *blessings*—not mere disciplines, but channels through which God gives us spiritual food for our survival, growth, and flourishing in the mission.

For more than a generation now, we have seen a renewal of interest among Christians in the spiritual disciplines. There has

---

[13] Rigney's book, then, also focuses on two of the three: indirect godwardness and corporate godwardness. Corporate godwardness is the category our projects share in common, while the respective direct or indirect focus makes them distinct. I eagerly send you to Rigney's book to consider how "the things of earth" can serve as (general) means of God's grace.

been much good in this renewal. But too many have emphasized technique and skill, with the unfortunate diminishing, or neglect, of God's role as supplier and provider. Too often the stress has been on the individual's initiative and effort, with little said about the place of the church and the corporate nature of God's plan. Much has been said in terms of duty, and too little said about joy. And the seeming proliferation of long lists of disciplines can leave young Christians overwhelmed by what they're not practicing, and in some cases contribute to a low-grade sense of guilt which threatens to keep us from fully engaging with the rest of our everyday lives for which these practices should be preparing us.

My hope in reshifting the focus from the spiritual disciplines to the means of grace—and then the various personal habits of grace that we develop in light of them—is to keep the gospel and the energy of God at the center, to draw in the essential (and often neglected) corporate aspect, and to simplify the way we think about these practices (as hearing God's voice, having his ear, and belonging to his body). My prayer is that this approach will help to make the means of grace, and your own habits that develop around them, not just accessible and realistic but truly God's means of your knowing and enjoying Jesus.

Part 1

HEAR HIS VOICE

Word

Chapter 1

Shape Your Life with the Words of Life

The Christian life, from start to finish, is utterly dependent on the grace of God. Not only do we come into spiritual life by sheer grace (Acts 18:27; Rom. 3:24; Eph. 2:5), but it is in divine grace that we continue on (Acts 13:43). It is by God's grace that our souls survive through many trials (2 Cor. 12:9; Heb. 4:16), are strengthened for everyday life (2 Tim. 2:1; Heb. 13:9), and grow into greater maturity and health (2 Pet. 3:18).

And it is God's grace that enables us to make choices and expend effort to seek more of God (1 Cor. 15:10). It is a gift that we would have the desire for and take action to avail ourselves of the means of God's grace—his voice (the word), his ear (prayer), and his people (fellowship)—with the most basic principle of grace being the immersing of our lives in his word.

The Word Original

Before we identify the presence of God's voice in our lives with the many good habits of taking in his word—whether Bible reading and study, hearing sermons, Scripture meditation and memorization, and more—first let's see his word as a general principle, rather than the specific practices.

Before printing it and binding it and covering it with leather, consider the concept of God's word. *God speaks.* He reveals himself to us. He communicates with us. His word, as John Frame says, is "his powerful, authoritative self-expression."[1] Just as the words of a friend are central in revealing his person to us, so it is with God.

The one who created us—and sustains us moment by moment (Col. 1:17; Heb. 1:3)—has expressed himself to us in human words, and it is vital that we listen. The other principal means of his grace (prayer and fellowship), while equally essential, are not as fundamental as this one. Creation (Gen. 1:3) and new creation (2 Cor. 4:6) both begin with the voice of God. He initiates, and does so by speaking. This self-expression of God is so deep and rich and full that it is not just personal, but a person.

The Word Incarnate

The complete and climactic self-revelation of God to man is the God-man, his Son (Heb. 1:1–2). Jesus is "the Word" (John 1:1), and "the Word became flesh" (John 1:14). He is the one who most fully and finally "has made [the Father] known" (John 1:18). Jesus is God's culminating self-expression, and says without any sham or embellishment, "Whoever has seen me has seen the Father" (John 14:9).

Jesus is the Word of God embodied. He is the grace of God incarnate (Titus 2:11). So full and complete is his revealing of God that *he* is not a word-thing, but a Word-person. He fulfilled the destiny of humanity in his perfect life and sacrificial

---

[1] This is a common refrain in Frame's corpus, but the main source would be his book-length treatment in *The Doctrine of the Word of God* (Phillipsburg, NJ: P&R, 2010).

death (Heb. 2:9), and rose again in triumph over sin and death, and now sits at the Father's right hand, with all things being put in subjection to him (1 Cor. 15:25–28). He is the divine-human Word our souls need for survival and strength and growth. But how do we access this Word now that he sits in heaven?

The Word Evangelical

The most frequent use of *word* in the New Testament is in reference to the message of the gospel—*the word evangelical* we might call it, or *the gospel word*—the message about Jesus, "the word of Christ" (Col. 3:16). For Paul, the phrases "preach Christ" and "proclaim Christ" and "speak *the word*" are synonymous (Phil. 1:14–17). The mission of his life, Paul says, is "to testify to the gospel of the grace of God" (Acts 20:24), which is "*the word* of his grace" (Acts 20:32).

It is "the word of truth, the gospel" that not only comes to us for conversion but also bears fruit and grows (Col. 1:5). It is "the word of truth, the gospel of your salvation" that changes everything for Christians (Eph. 1:13), and "the word of life" to which we hold fast in the midst of a crooked and perverse society (Phil. 2:15–16). And so, in the Christian fight for joy, John Piper writes, "The central strategy is to preach the gospel to yourself. . . . Hearing the word of the cross, and preaching it to ourselves, is the central strategy for sinners in the fight for joy."[2]

And as this gospel-word passes from mouth to mouth, from person to person, from people to people, from nation to nation, how will *the message* about Jesus stay on message? What will keep the spoken word faithful and true and life-changing? And how do we keep ourselves from falling into ruts and from defaulting to the same old canned ways of telling the message?

---

[2] *When I Don't Desire God: How to Fight for Joy* (Wheaton, IL: Crossway, 2004), 81, 91. More at the end of this chapter on preaching the gospel to yourself.

The Word Written

Having spied the pinnacle of God's Word in the person and work of Jesus, and the prevalence of God's word in his gospel, now we come to the essential place, this side of heaven, for God's word written. Just as crucial as it is for spiritual life that we have God in his Word Jesus, and that we have Jesus in his word the gospel, so we need the Scriptures as God's inspired, inerrant, and infallible revelation of himself.

Without the Bible, we will soon lose the genuine gospel and the real Jesus and the true God. For now, if we are to saturate our lives with the words of life, we must be people of the Book. Which is no necessary prescription to every Christian for the same particular habits. But it is a summons to the principle of soaking our lives in the voice of God and diversifying the portfolio of access points. Before pondering the many and wonderful habits of grace that might be best for you in your context and season of life, put this rock in place: Fashion rhythms of life that help you revolve around having God's incarnate Word, by God's gospel word, through God's written word.

The Word Pervasive

With such a perspective on God's word in place, countless creative routines may follow, whether it's reading through the Bible in a year, or memorizing passages or whole books, or meditating on single verses or paragraphs, or aggressively identifying and pursuing applications, or listening to sermon podcasts, or reading biblically rich content online, or taking Bible classes, or consuming Christian books, and on and on—and changing it up from time to time. The potential practices are limitless, but the principle beneath the practices is this: The fundamental means of God's ongoing grace, through his Spirit, in the life of the Christian and the life of the church is God's self-expression in his Word, in the gospel, perfectly kept for us and on display in all its textures, riches, and hues in the external written word of the Scriptures.

As we consider Bible reading, study, meditation, memorization, application, and lifelong learning in the coming chapters—and most importantly, sitting under faithful Bible preaching, which comes in part 3—may God give you intentionality to shape your weeks with his word, ingenuity to shower your days with his voice, and creativity to punctuate your life and the lives of those around you with fresh routines for regularly availing yourself of his life-giving words.

———

More on Preaching to Yourself

Before moving on to consider Bible intake in some of its many forms, let's circle back and say more about preaching the gospel to ourselves and its function as a means of grace. After all, we saw above from Piper: "Hearing the word of the cross, and preaching it to ourselves, is the central strategy for sinners in the fight for joy."[3]

In our sin, we constantly find our responses to life in our fallen world to be disconnected from the theology that we confess. Anger, fear, panic, discouragement, and impatience stalk our hearts and whisper in our ears a false gospel that will lure our lives away from what we say we believe. The battleground is between our ears. What is it that is capturing your idle thoughts? What fear or frustration is filling your spare moments? Will you just listen to yourself, or will you start talking?

[3] Ibid., 91.

No, preaching—not letting your concerns shape you, but forming your concerns by the power of the gospel.

Preaching the gospel to ourselves is a habit of grace that is both proactive and reactive. It's reactive as we encounter temptation and frustration and seek to restock in the moment, or as we reflect back on our sin and circumstances and try to evaluate them with a gospel lens. But it's also proactive. We go on the offensive when we feed our souls in some regular rhythm before the events and tasks and disappointments of daily life begin streaming our way.

There is a difference between merely reminding ourselves of truth and preaching to ourselves the truth of the gospel. It's true that two plus two equals four. But it does very little to feed our souls. What we need is not just truth, but *the* truth, the message of the gospel. What preaching the gospel to ourselves requires is pausing, rehearsing some expression of the Father's and Son's love and provision of goodness and rescue and joy for us, and consciously seeking to have that truth shape and permeate our reality.

As it relates to Scripture, it is important to note that gospel self-preaching is not the same thing as Bible reading, though the connections and interdependences are profound. The Scriptures, in one sense, provide the material for preaching to ourselves the gospel of grace. They are the content to be taken up and applied to our lives in view of Jesus's person and work.

It will not adequately strengthen our soul, in the long run, just to hear the same canned gospel repeated over and over. Neither will it sustain our spiritual lives to merely take in information without seeing it in light of Jesus, and pressing it into our hearts.[4]

---

[4] For a list of ten one-sentence "gospel verses" and twelve short "gospel passages," see the end of chapter 5, pages 75–81. For more on the relationship between Bible intake and preaching to yourself, see David Mathis and Jonathan Parnell, *How to Stay Christian in Seminary* (Wheaton, IL: Crossway, 2014), 38–40.

Chapter 2

Read for Breadth,
Study for Depth

There is some science to good Bible reading. It's important to know the fundamentals of language and communication, of subjects and verbs and objects and conjunctions. Much can be gained from boning up on some basics of English or doing some reading about reading.[1] It's helpful to have good Bible study aids, like overviews, introductions, and reliable commentaries (especially for the Old Testament prophets), and to have a good sense of how the Scriptures are put together as a whole.

And just like we learn to ride a bike with training wheels, it can help to have someone spell out some simple method of "inductive Bible study" with the dance steps of observation, interpretation, and application. Rudimentary, memorable approaches like this abound in Christian circles serious about the Bible. They are a gift to help us get going and come to an otherwise dauntingly large book with some idea of what to do next.

---

[1] For instance, Mortimer Adler and Charles Van Doren, *How to Read a Book: The Classic Guide to Intelligent Reading* (New York: Touchstone, 1972) and Tony Reinke, *Lit! A Christian Guide to Reading Books* (Wheaton, IL: Crossway, 2011).

But the point of learning the little bits of science behind it all is to be ready to dance when the music begins to play. And the best of dancing isn't just taught in classrooms, but caught in practice.

Good Bible reading is no mere science; it is an art. The Bible itself is a special compilation of great artistries. And the best way to learn the art of reading the Bible for yourself is this: *Read it for yourself.*

Ask an Old Saint

Ask an old, weathered saint who's been reading the Scriptures for himself for decades. See if he has a nice, clean formulation for how he goes about his daily reading. Does he have three or four simple, memorable steps he walks through consciously each day? The answer likely will be no; he's learned over time there's more art to it than that.

Or more generally, just ask, How do you go about reading the Bible? You might see it on his face that it's a tough question to answer. Not because there aren't some basic, little "scientific" things, like the basics of reading and comprehension, or the various patterns and methods he's developed for feeding his own soul over the years, but because he's learned that so much of good Bible reading is an art. It's a skill learned in engaging the task, not mainly sitting under formal instruction. And those who have read their Bibles most are the ones who have learned the craft best.

Learn the Art through Practice

No biblical author gives us any nice, clean acrostic for how to go about daily Bible reading. And you won't find one in this chapter. That may feel daunting for the beginner who wants assistance, but in the long run it proves wonderfully freeing.

It can be a great help to have training wheels for a season, but once you learn to ride the bike, those extra things sticking out the side are terribly constrictive and limiting.

At the end of the day, there is simply no replacement for finding a regular time and place, blocking out distractions, putting your nose in the text, and letting your mind and heart be led and captured and thrilled by God himself communicating to us in his objective written words.

If you feel uncomfortable in the Scriptures and inadequate in the art of Bible reading, the single most important thing you can do is make a regular habit of reading the Bible for yourself. There is no substitute for a few focused minutes each day in the text. You may be surprised how much the little bits add up over the long haul.

As much as we want a quick fix, some fast lesson that makes us near-experts in just a few short minutes, the best of Bible reading isn't learned overnight or even after a semester of lectures, but day after day, week after week, month after month, and year after year, imbibing the Bible, having God's words inform our minds, inspire our hearts, instruct our lives. It is then that we slowly see the lights going on everywhere as we walk through life, and keep walking through the texts.

Discover the Art of Meditation

One piece of counsel for any Bible reading plan, however ambitious, is this: Don't let the push to check boxes keep you from lingering over a text, whether to seek to understand it ("study") or to emotionally glory in what you understand ("meditation").

Think of your Bible reading as a regular surveying of the biblical landscape to find a spot to settle down for a few moments to meditate, which is the high point and richest moment of Bible intake (more on meditation in the next chapter). Go for breadth (in reading) and depth (in study), where you stop at something you don't understand, pose questions and give answers, consult resources, and perhaps capture a brief reflection in words or a diagram. There is a place in Bible reading for "raking" and gathering up the leaves at a swift pace, but when we "dig" in Bible study, we unearth the diamonds. In meditation, we marvel at the jewels.

Bible reading is like watching the film in real time. Study is like going through a clip frame by frame. Meditation, then, along with Scripture memory (chap. 5), is for lingering over particular frames and pressing the significance to our hearts and into our lives.

Grow in Finding Jesus

One final thing to say about Bible reading as art, not just science, is that Jesus taught his apostles to read the Scriptures in what we might describe as an artistic way. The science part of Bible reading is essential, but it doesn't necessitate reading so rigidly, narrowly, and modernistically that only the most explicit and specific of prophecies apply to Christ, or that the text is always "for the original readers" and never really for us.

Jesus himself read the Scriptures with much more flair—not in any way making things up, but seeing with the eyes of faith what's really there to be seen below the surface, out of sight to the natural mind. Such deep reading is a kind of acquired taste, through regular practice, not an easily transferred skill; it's developing the apostolic palate for finding Jesus throughout the Scriptures, by tracking the trajectory of God's grace, in its many textures and tones, without falling into either unbelief or make-believe. It is learning with the apostle John that "the testimony of Jesus is the spirit of prophecy" (Rev. 19:10).

And so "beginning with Moses and all the Prophets," Jesus himself "interpreted to them in all the Scriptures the things concerning himself" (Luke 24:27). He claimed, "Abraham rejoiced that he would see my day. He saw it and was glad" (John 8:56). He said Moses "wrote of me" (John 5:46), and that "everything written about me in the Law of Moses and the Prophets and the Psalms must be fulfilled" (Luke 24:44). And so he opened their minds—beyond their narrow, fallen rationality—to truly understand the Scriptures (Luke 24:45).

As we learn to read the Bible not only with our left brains but with our whole minds and hearts, we see more and more how the apostles heard the whispers of the Scriptures—and how they saw pointers to Jesus everywhere.

Resolved: To Read the Bible

Whether you feel like a beginner or the grizzled old veteran, one of the most important things you can do is regularly read the Bible for yourself.

It is a remarkable thing that we have Bibles we can read personally, whenever we want. For most of church history, and still today in many places in the world, Christians have not had their own personal copies of the Bible. They had to gather to hear someone read it to them. "Devote yourself to the public reading of Scripture" (1 Tim. 4:13) was all they had, other than memory, for Bible intake.

But now, with printed Bibles and electronic options galore, we have priceless access to God's very words to us, words that we are so tragically tempted to take lightly. Reading your own copy of the Bible daily is not a law that every believer must abide; most Christians have not had this option. But the habit of daily Bible reading can be a marvelous means of God's grace. Why miss this bounty and blessing?

The Whole Thing?

"All Scripture," says 2 Timothy 3:16, "is breathed out by God and profitable." Everything in Scripture, from Genesis 1 to

Revelation 22, is for the good of the church. "Now these things happened to them as an example, but they were written down *for our instruction*, on whom the end of the ages has come" (1 Cor. 10:11). "Whatever was written in former days was written *for our instruction*, that through endurance and through the encouragement of the Scriptures we might have hope" (Rom. 15:4).

But not every text functions to build our faith in the same way or has the same effect for every one of God's children in the new covenant. It is a wonderful thing to read all the way through the Bible. It is something that pastors and teachers in the church should strongly consider doing on an annual basis, to let all the Scriptural data pass before their eyes for continually informing their public theological claims. But this is not a yoke to be set on every Christian every year. (Though it would be a good thing for every Christian to try at some point, or at least to have some multiyear plan in place to eventually get you through the whole Bible in some cycle.)

For those considering the journey, you may be surprised how doable it is. It takes about seventy hours to read the Bible from cover to cover. "That's less time than the average American spends in front of the television every month," observes Donald S. Whitney. "In other words, if most people would exchange their TV time for Scripture reading, they'd finish reading the entire Bible in four weeks or less. If that sounds unworkable, consider this: In no more than fifteen minutes a day you can read through the Bible in less than a year's time."[2]

Maybe this coming new year, or even now, is your time to set out on the journey. Some of my favorite Bible reading plans over the years have been M'Cheyne and The Kingdom, along with my most beloved from *Discipleship Journal*.[3]

---

[2] *Spiritual Disciplines for the Christian Life*, rev. ed. (Colorado Springs: NavPress, 2014), 29.
[3] M'Cheyne's Bible reading plan is available online at http://www.edginet.org/mcheyne /printables.html; The Kingdom, developed by Jason DeRouchie, at http://cdn.desiringgod .org/pdf/blog/3325_FINAL.DeRouchie.pdf; and *Discipleship Journal*'s, by the Naviga-

Or if the whole thing in one year seems out of your reach, try taking up a plan and working through it at your own pace, even if it takes you several years. It will give you a specific place to go next when you open the Bible, instead of just opening to some random text, and in time it will give you confidence that you've traversed the whole terrain of Scripture and at least glimpsed all God's full written revelation to us.

More Than Just Raking

So far we've been talking about Bible reading. The habit of reading just a few minutes a day can get us a long way in a relatively short time. But when we slow down and study, we soon find out we have more than a life's work ahead of us. Study is hard work. The difference between reading and study makes me think of yard work.

Raking is relatively easy work and can make the yard look better in a short time. It's easy enough that even three-year-olds can help, thanks to a kids' rake from the neighborhood hardware store.

Raking may make my back a little sore the next day, but it's nothing like the digging we did to prepare our front yard for a small retaining wall. Raking, even a lot of it, is reasonably painless. Digging, even just a small amount, can be backbreaking. But moving earth can be gloriously rewarding. It can do a lot more to improve a yard than just collecting the leaves—though my soft side still would take the rake anytime.

Digging in Divine Words

So both reading and study have their place in Bible intake, and we need to periodically remind ourselves to slow down, bore in, and go deep when reading the Bible. No doubt, some Christians naturally incline to a slower gear, and they need the reminder to press forward for breadth, keep the larger context in view, and reflect on the big picture, not just individual verses as little lozenges for the soul.

But others of us tend to coast toward raking. It takes less energy, especially early in the morning before the coffee has kicked in, to just keep reading, skimming along the surface of the text, rather than slowing down, asking questions, and perhaps even capturing some brief reflections. In a minute flat, we can be done with another chapter and ready to check the box. It feels more challenging to pick up a pencil, or to open a laptop and go straight to an empty document for recording thoughts without getting sidetracked into e-mail, social media, or whatever else.

Getting Better at Bible Study

For the Christian seeking to develop the ability to feed his soul with God's words, there is simply no replacement for diving in daily. Yes, you can pick up some skills and techniques here or there, in a classroom or in a book on Bible study. But you don't need seminary to feast regularly in the Scriptures. Most of the world's best Bible readers and appliers have little formal training, if any.

It's like any sport. There's no substitute for getting yourself on the field and in the game. You can talk about it only for so long until the only way to really improve is to actually play. Listening to gifted, insightful preachers and teachers is critical. Using good references provides important aid.[4] But there

---

[4] I recommend *ESV Study Bible*, ed. Wayne Grudem et al. (Wheaton, IL: Crossway, 2008); D. A. Carson and Douglas J. Moo, *An Introduction to the New Testament*, 2nd ed. (Grand Rapids, MI: Zondervan, 2005); Tremper Longman III and Raymond B. Dillard, *An Introduction to the Old Testament*, 2nd ed. (Grand Rapids, MI: Zondervan, 2006).

is simply no stand-in for studying the Scriptures for ourselves, and doing so for the long haul.

Don't Forget Your Shovel

As we aim to feed ourselves daily from the inexhaustible pantry, we need a diet of both breadth and depth. There's a place for reading whole Bible books in one sitting and a place for going deep in half a verse. It takes both an increasing sense of the big picture of Jesus's rescue of sinners as well as a growing depth in the little pieces that make up that big picture for us to stay fresh in applying the gospel to our lives.

Without raking, we won't have enough sense of the landscape to dig in the right places. And without digging, and making sure the banner of our theology is securely tethered to specific biblical sentences and paragraphs, our resources will soon dry up for feeding our souls with various grains and tastes.

Discover the Diamonds

In the introduction to his book *Future Grace*, John Piper celebrates the place of "unrushed reflection," and asks the reader to make space for it.

> O the riches of understanding that come from lingering in thought over a new idea—or a new expression of an old idea! I would like this book to be read in the same way that the apostle Paul wanted his letters to be read by Timothy: "*Think over* what I say, for the Lord will give you understanding in everything" (2 Timothy 2:7).
>
> Every book worth reading beckons with the words, "*Think over* what I say." . . . When my sons complain that a book is too hard to read, I say, "Raking is easy, but all you get is leaves; digging is hard, but you might find diamonds."[5]

---

[5] *Future Grace: The Purifying Power of the Promises of God*, rev. ed. (Colorado Springs: Multnomah, 2012), 10.

And if this is true for every book worth reading, how much more so for God's Book. Let's rake for breadth and gather the leaves. And let's dig for depth and look for the diamonds too.

———

The X Factor in Bible Reading

Before closing this chapter on Bible reading and study, there is one important, mysterious subject to raise. We might call it the X factor in Bible reading and study.

The Bible is no magic book, but a strange, enigmatic power stirs when we reach for the Scriptures. Something influential, though invisible, is happening as we hear God's words read or spoken, and when we read or study. Something supernatural, but unseen, transpires as we see the text in front of us and take it into our souls. Someone unseen moves.

He is a personal force, fully divine and full of mystery—more a person than you or me, and yet no less an indomitable and ultimately irresistible power. He makes the seemingly simple into something supernatural, as reading the Bible takes us beyond the realm of our control.

He loves to strengthen human souls in obvious and subtle ways as they encounter God's word—whether that Word is the incarnate Christ, the gospel word of salvation for sinners, or the written word in the Scriptures.

As much as we want to master the habit of Bible intake, to trace the lines of cause and effect from some action we take to some resulting satisfaction of our soul, the Helper resists our efforts to objectify grace. He lingers in silence. He labors mysteriously, outside our control. He imperceptibly shapes us this morning to make us into who we need to be this afternoon, and next week. His hands act untraceably as he molds our minds, hews out our hearts, whittles at our wills, and carves at our calluses.

He not only hovers over the waters (Gen. 1:2) and over all created space, standing ready to execute the Father's will and extend the reign of the glorified Son. He also hovers with special vigilance over the divine word—whether incarnate, spoken, or written—standing ready to awaken dead souls and open blind eyes and warm cold hearts. Ready to bear witness about the Son (John 15:26), ready to glorify him (John 16:14).

It was by this Helper that the gospel first came to us "not only in word, but also in power" (1 Thess. 1:5), and it was with his joy that we "received the word in much affliction" (1 Thess. 1:6). It was by him that "God chose [us] . . . to be saved, through sanctification" (2 Thess. 2:13).

With him in view, Jesus said to the Samaritan woman, "The hour is coming, and is now here, when the true worshipers will worship the Father in spirit and truth, for the Father is seeking such people to worship him. God is spirit, and those who worship him must worship in spirit and truth" (John 4:23–24).

He is the one through whom now is revealed to us the "secret and hidden wisdom of God, which God decreed before the ages for our glory" (1 Cor. 2:7–10). Our Helper is the one who searches everything, even the depths of God (1 Cor. 2:10). No one comprehends the thoughts of God, except our Aide (1 Cor. 2:11). He is the one whom the truly born again have received "that we might understand the things freely given us by God" (1 Cor. 2:12). And so when we communicate the Christian message and teaching, we "impart this in words not taught by human wisdom," but taught by him, "interpreting spiritual truths to those who are spiritual" (1 Cor. 2:13).

He is the promised One, with whom we were sealed when we "heard the word of truth, the gospel of your salvation, and believed in [Jesus]" (Eph. 1:13). The word of God is said to be his sword (Eph. 6:17).

When we get alone with the Bible, we are not alone. God has not left us to ourselves to understand his words and feed our own souls. No matter how thin your training, no matter how spotty your routine, the Helper stands ready. Take up the text in confidence that God is primed to bless your being with his very breath.

There is more than meets the eye to Bible reading and study as habits of grace. There is a variable we can't control. An enigmatic power we cannot command. A mysterious goodness we can only receive.

He is the Holy Spirit.

Chapter 3

Warm Yourself at the Fire of Meditation

We were made to meditate. God designed us with the capacity to pause and ponder. He means for us to not just hear him, not only to read quickly over what he says, but to reflect on what he says and knead it into our hearts.

It is a distinctively human trait to stop and consider, to chew on something with the teeth of our minds and hearts, to roll some reality around in our thoughts and press it deeply into our feelings, to look from different angles and seek to get a better sense of its significance.

The biblical name for this art is *meditation*, which Donald S. Whitney defines as "deep thinking on the truths and spiritual realities revealed in Scripture for the purposes of understanding, application, and prayer."[1] It is a marvelous means of God's grace in the Christian life—perhaps the most misunderstood, and most underrated, of the disciplines in the church today. And it is the high point of receiving God's word.

---

[1] *Spiritual Disciplines for the Christian Life*, rev. ed. (Colorado Springs: NavPress, 2014), 46.

Meditation Made Christian

Since we were made to meditate, we shouldn't be surprised to find that world religions have seized upon the activity, and new schools try to make use of its practical effects, whether to cultivate brain health or lower blood pressure. Christian meditation, however, is fundamentally different from the "meditation" popularly co-opted by various non-Christian systems. It doesn't entail emptying our minds, but rather filling them with biblical and theological substance—truth outside of ourselves—and then chewing on that content, until we begin to feel some of its magnitude in our hearts.

For the Christian, meditation means having "the word of Christ dwell in you richly" (Col. 3:16). It is not, like secular meditation, "doing nothing and being tuned in to your own mind at the same time," but it is feeding our minds on the words of God and digesting them slowly, savoring the texture, enjoying the juices, cherishing the flavor of such rich fare. Meditation that is truly Christian is guided by the gospel, shaped by the Scriptures, reliant upon the Holy Spirit, and exercised in faith.

Man does not live by bread alone, and meditation is slowly relishing the meal.

Meditation Day and Night

Maybe it's the multiplied distractions of modern life, and the increased impairments of sin's corruption, but meditation is more the lost art today than it was for our fathers in the faith. We are told, "Isaac went out to meditate in the field toward evening" (Gen. 24:63), and three of the more important texts in the Hebrew Scriptures, among others, call for meditation in such a way that we should sit up and take notice—or better, slow down, block out distractions, and give it some serious consideration.

The first is Joshua 1:8. At a key juncture in redemptive history, following the death of Moses, God himself speaks to Joshua, and three times gives the clear directive, "Be strong and courageous" (Josh. 1:6, 7, 9). How is he to do this? Where will he fill his tank with such strength and courage? Meditation. "This Book of the Law shall not depart from your mouth, but you shall *meditate on it day and night*" (Josh. 1:8).

God means not for Joshua to be merely familiar with the Book, or that he read through sections of it quickly in the morning, or even just that he go deep in it in study, but that he be captivated by it and build his life on its truths. His spare thoughts should go there, his idle mind gravitate there. God's words of instruction are to saturate his life, give him direction, shape his mind, form his patterns, fuel his affections, and inspire his actions.

Meditation in the Psalms

Two more key texts come in the first Psalm and the longest. Psalm 1:1–2 echoes the language of Joshua 1, "Blessed is the man . . . [whose] delight is in the law of the LORD, and on his law he meditates day and night." The blessed one, the happy one, who delights in God's word, doesn't avail himself of the words of life merely with some quick breadth reading, punctuated with blocks of study, but "meditates day and night."

And meditation nearly dominates Psalm 119 and its celebration of the words of God, as the psalmist says he meditates "on your precepts" (vv. 15 and 78), "on your statutes" (vv. 23 and 48), and "on your wondrous works" (v. 27). He claims, "Your testimonies are my meditation" (v. 99) and exclaims, "Oh how I love your law! It is my meditation all the day" (v. 97). If God's old-covenant instruction could be so precious to the psalmist, how much more should the new-covenant gospel captivate our meditation.

Meditation Is the Missing Link

Meditation on the Scriptures has occupied a deep and endur-
ing place in the history of the church as one of the mightiest
means of God's grace for his people. In particular, the Puritans
celebrated the gift of meditation as much as any, and drew attention to its vital relationship with hearing God's voice (Bible
intake) and having his ear (prayer). Whitney catalogs several
prominent Puritans to the effect that meditation is "the miss-
ing link between Bible intake and prayer," and in doing so, he
moves us into some practical counsel for Christian meditation:[2]

- "Begin with reading or hearing. Go on with meditation;
  end in prayer." (William Bridge, "The Work and the Way
  of Meditation")
- "The word feedeth meditation, and meditation feedeth
  prayer. . . . Meditation must follow hearing and precede
  prayer. . . . What we take in by the word we digest by meditation and let out by prayer." (Thomas Manton, *Complete
  Works*, vol. 17)
- "The reason we come away so cold from reading the word
  is, because we do not warm ourselves at the fire of meditation." (Thomas Watson, "How We May Read the Scriptures with Most Spiritual Profit," dir. 8)
- "The great reason why our prayers are ineffectual, is because we do not meditate before them." (William Bates,
  "On Divine Meditation," chap. 4)

Meditation, then, for the Christian, is a discipline that has a
certain function related to the other disciplines. It doesn't stand
alone, hermetically sealed from God's revelation of himself in
the Bible and our reverential response to him in prayer. Rather,

---

[2] Ibid., 86–93. Meditation as a "bridge discipline" between hearing from God in his word and
responding to him in prayer is also a major theme in Timothy Keller, *Prayer: Experiencing Awe
and Intimacy with God* (New York: Dutton, 2014).

meditation bridges the gap between hearing from God and speaking to him.

In meditation, we pause and reflect over his words, which we have read, heard, or studied. We roll them over in our minds and let them ignite our hearts—we "warm ourselves at the fire of meditation." We go deep in God's revelation, take it into our very souls, and as we are being changed by his truth, we respond to him in prayer. As Matthew Henry says, "As meditation is the best preparation for prayer, so prayer is the best issue of meditation."[3]

True Healing

Christian meditation is less about the posture of our bodies and more about the posture of our souls. Our instructions aren't, sit on the floor with your legs crossed, or sit on a chair with both feet on the floor and your back straight, palms facing upward. Christian meditation begins with our eyes in the Book, or ears open to the word, or a mind stocked with memorized Scripture.

Perhaps we start with some broader Bible reading from which we select a particular verse or phrase that caught our attention, and carve out several minutes to go deep in it. Then, with intentionality and focus—often best with pen in hand or fingers on the keys—we seek to better understand God's words and warm our soul at his fire, and let it lead us into prayer and then into the day.

In our restless and stressed-out society, it very well may strengthen our brain and lower our blood pressure to practice the art of Christian meditation. But even more significant will be the good that it does for our souls.

---

[3] Quoted in Donald S. Whitney, *Spiritual Disciplines for the Christian Life*, rev. ed. (Colorado Springs: NavPress, 2014), 88.

―――――

The High Point of Daily Devotions

I think of meditation as the high point of my daily devotional time. After beginning with a brief prayer for God's help, I read through the assigned passages for the day in a Bible-reading plan. As I read, I'm on the lookout for how the passage relates to Jesus, and whether there are phrases, verses, or sections that capture my attention for meditation or study. If study, and it's just a quick question, I can check cross references or a commentary or study Bible note. If the question is more involved, I make a note for more extended study at some later time that day or week, rather than letting it sidetrack my morning devotional time. (Some of these notes for study, I come back to later and look into further; some I don't find time for and leave till the next time I come across that text in my reading.)

If I come across a section of Scripture during my reading that inspires me for meditation, I may simply linger there, and then transition into prayer and into the day, without feeling any need to return to reading the remainder of the assigned passages. I remind myself over and over that it's not about checking boxes but communing with God in his word through meditation and into prayer. In a way, I think of the assigned passages as biblical fodder for satisfying my soul with meditation and serving as a bridge into prayer.

Chapter 4

Bring the Bible Home
to Your Heart

─────

We all want to be "doers of the word, and not hearers only" (James 1:22). Who wants to feel the failure or share in the shame of being pegged like one "who looks intently at his natural face in a mirror . . . and goes away and at once forgets what he was like" (James 1:23–24)? It would seem like Bible application is an essential spiritual discipline to consciously pursue every time we encounter God's word—but that depends on how we define "application."

The key question we need to answer in this chapter is what effect should regular Bible intake have on our hearts and lives—and *how* does it happen?

God's Word Is for You

For starters, we should be clear that aiming to apply God's words to our lives is grounded in the good instinct that *the Bible is for us*. Optimism about life application makes good on these amazing claims that *all the Scriptures* are for Christians:

- "All Scripture is breathed out by God and profitable for teaching, for reproof, for correction, and for training in righteousness, that the man of God may be complete, equipped for every good work" (2 Tim. 3:16–17).
- "Now these things took place as examples for us, that we might not desire evil as they did. . . . They were written down for our instruction, on whom the end of the ages has come" (1 Cor. 10:6, 11).
- "Whatever was written in former days was written for our instruction, that through endurance and through the encouragement of the Scriptures we might have hope" (Rom. 15:4).

The whole Bible is for the whole church. We have good scriptural warrant to come to God's words expecting them to be understandable and applicable. We should make good on Puritan preacher Thomas Watson's counsel when we open the Book,

> Take every word as spoken to yourselves. When the word thunders against sin, think thus: "God means my sins;" when it presseth any duty, "God intends me in this." Many put off Scripture from themselves, as if it only concerned those who lived in the time when it was written; but if you intend to profit by the word, bring it home to yourselves: a medicine will do no good, unless it be applied.[1]

Yes, take every word as spoken to yourself, with this essential anchor in place: Seek to understand first how God's words fell on the original hearers, and how they relate to Jesus's person and work, and then bring them home to yourself. Expect application to your life as God speaks to us today through the Spirit-illumined understanding of what the inspired human author said to his original readers in the biblical text.

---

[1] Quoted in Donald S. Whitney, *Spiritual Disciplines for the Christian Life*, rev. ed. (Colorado Springs: NavPress, 2014), 71.

Specific Applications for Every Day?

So then, is it right to think of "application" as an everyday means of God's grace? Is this a spiritual discipline to be pursued with every Bible encounter? The answer is yes and no, depending on what we mean by *application*.

Some good teachers say that every encounter with God's word should include at least one specific application to our lives—some particular addition, however small, to who we are or to our daily to-do list. There is a wise intention in this: pressing ourselves to be not just hearers of God's word, but doers. But such a simplistic approach to application overlooks the more complex nature of the Christian life—and how true and lasting change happens in a less straightforward way than we may be prone to think.

It helps to acknowledge that the vast majority of our lives are lived spontaneously. More than 99 percent of our daily decisions about this and that happen without any immediate reflection. We just act. Our lives flow from the kind of person we are—the kind of person we have become—rather than some succession of time-outs for reflection.

And this is precisely the line along which the apostle prays for us. He asks not that God give us simple obedience to a clear to-do list of commands, but that he give us wisdom to discern his will as we encounter life's many choices coming at us without pause. Paul prays

- that you would be "transformed by the renewal of your mind, that by testing you may discern what is the will of God, what is good and acceptable and perfect" (Rom. 12:2);
- that your love may "abound more and more, with knowledge and all discernment, so that you may approve what is excellent" (Phil. 1:9–10);

- that you "may be filled with the knowledge of his will in all spiritual wisdom and understanding, so as to walk in a manner worthy of the Lord, fully pleasing to him, bearing fruit in every good work and increasing in the knowledge of God" (Col. 1:9–10).

Rather than dictating specific actions, the apostle wants to see us formed into the kind of persons who are able to "discern what is pleasing to the Lord" (Eph. 5:10), and then act in light of it.

God's Word Is for Seeing

And so, as John Piper says, "A godly life is lived out of an astonished heart—a heart that is astonished at grace. We go to the Bible to be astonished, to be amazed at God and Christ and the cross and grace and the gospel."[2] The kind of application most important to pursue in encountering God's word is such astonishment. Press the Scriptures to your soul. Pray for the awakening of your affections. Bring the Bible home to your heart. It's really just another way of commending meditation.

As we're freshly captivated by the grandeur of our God and his gospel, we become what we behold: "We all, with unveiled face, beholding the glory of the Lord, are being transformed into the same image from one degree of glory to another" (2 Cor. 3:18). And so we come away from our Bible intake with a more satisfied soul, which imparts a flavor and demeanor to our lives and decision-making that affects everything.

Meditating on God's words shapes our soul. Sometimes it yields immediate and specific points of application—embrace them when they come. But be careful not to let the drive for specific actions alter the focus of our devotions from astonishment and seeking to have your soul happy in the Lord. Coming

---

[2] "Must Bible Reading Always End with Application?," *Ask Pastor John*, episode 26, desiring God.org, February 13, 2013, http://www.desiringgod.org/interviews/must-bible-reading-always-end-with-application.

to the Scriptures to see and feel makes for a drastically different approach than primarily coming to do.

The Bible is gloriously for us, but it is not mainly about us. We come most deeply because of *whom* we will see, not for what we must do. "Become a kind of person," counsels Piper, "don't amass a long list."[3]

The Blessing of Bringing It Home

This is the pathway to flourishing we catch a glimpse of in the old covenant in Joshua 1:8—meditation, then application, then blessing:

> This Book of the Law shall not depart from your mouth, but you shall meditate on it day and night, so that you may be careful to do according to all that is written in it. For then you will make your way prosperous, and then you will have good success.

When Bible reading first aims at astonishment (meditation and worship), it works first on our hearts and changes our person, which then prepares us for application. And application of God's words to our lives prepares us for God's blessing of our souls: "Your way [will be] prosperous, and then you will have good success." So applying God's words to our lives is not only an effect of his grace to us, but also a means to more grace.

Jesus says in John 13:17, "If you know these things, blessed are you if you do them." So also James 1:25 promises that someone who is not a hearer only but "a doer who acts . . . will be blessed in his doing."

When we bring God's words home to our hearts, and then apply them to our lives through an amazed and changed heart, it is a great means of his grace to us. He loves to bless the true application of his word to our lives.

---

[3] Ibid.

Chapter 5

Memorize the Mind of God

Perhaps you've heard the pitch for Scripture memory a hundred times. You're persuaded the benefits would be incalculable, and that there may be no better use of your time than to hide God's word in your heart and store it away for future use. But you've tried your hand at it again and again, and just never got the magic working.

Maybe the thought of memorizing Scripture brings back some sentiment you can't shake from doing rote memorization in grade school, or eventually you've thrown up your hands and blamed your failures on a bad memory. You know it would be wonderful to have a store of Scripture treasured up, or an arsenal of weapons stockpiled for the Spirit's use. But if it is all oriented on saving up for some uncertain future time, and has little to do with today, you likely don't feel much urgency about it.

But maybe a breakthrough could come with some simple change in perspective. What if Scripture memory really is about today? At least for a minute, forget decades from now; throw aside the litany of daily reviews of previously memorized texts;

abandon the mentality of building the store and stocking the pile, at least as the driving motivation. Instead, focus on the present. Scripture memory, at its best, is about feeding your soul today and mapping your life and mind onto the very life and mind of God.

Mold Your Mind for Today

It's all well and good to store up bright treasures and sharp weapons for future use, but if you're cut from the cloth I am, you find it all too easy to put Scripture memory off when every today seems to already have enough trouble of its own (Matt. 6:34). Maybe the discovery you've needed to finally make some tracks is simply applying this line from the Lord's Prayer to Bible memorization: *Give us this day our daily bread* (Matt. 6:11).

When we learn the Scriptures by heart, we're not just memorizing ancient, enduringly relevant texts, but we're listening to and learning the voice of our Creator and Redeemer himself. When we memorize lines from the Bible, we are shaping our minds in the moment to mimic the structure and mind-set of the mind of God.

Good theology forms our minds in a general way to think God's thoughts after him. But memorized Scripture molds our minds, with as much specificity as is humanly possible, to mimic the folds and creases in the mind of God. Theology gets us to the ballpark; memorized Scripture, into the clubhouse.

And so Bible memory not only prepares us for the someday-maybes when we might use a memorized verse in counseling or witnessing or fighting sin, but it contributes powerfully in the present to making us the kind of person who walks in the Spirit today. It contributes right now to your being "renewed in the spirit of your minds" (Eph. 4:23) and being "transformed by the renewal of your mind, that by testing you may discern what is the will of God, what is good and acceptable and perfect" (Rom. 12:2). Not only might it then be accessible to us for future decision-making and temptation-battling in varying contexts, but the very act of memorizing Scripture, as we understand and engage with the meaning of the text, changes our minds in the present to make us the kind of people who "discern what is the will of God."

Memorizing God's words today, then, is not just a deposit into an account for tomorrow, but an asset working for us right now.

Some Call It "Meditation"

Note the disclaimer above: "as we understand and engage with the meaning of the text." That is, we must flood the process of memorization with the habit of grace and lost art we discussed in chapter 3: meditation.

There's nothing necessarily new age or transcendental about meditation. The old-school version, commended throughout the Bible, is thinking deeply about some truth from the mouth of God, and rolling it around in our minds long enough that we feel a sense of its significance in our hearts, and then even begin to envision its application in our lives. Making meditation work in tandem with Scripture memory has tremendous bearing on how we go about the arduous process of memorizing. For one, it makes us slow down. We can memorize things much faster if we don't pause to grasp and ponder. But mere memorization does us little good; meditation does much good. When we take meditation seriously, we seek not only to understand what we are memorizing, but also to linger over it, and feel it, and even begin to apply it as we memorize.

When we pursue Scripture memory with meditation, we're not just storing up for transformation later, but enjoying food for our soul today and experiencing transformation now. And when the focus is more on feeding and shaping, then constant review is less important. Once-memorized, now-forgotten texts aren't a tragedy, but an opportunity to meditate again freshly and mold your mind even more.

Reset Your Mind on the Things of the Spirit

Another important benefit today, not just in the future, is how Bible memory with meditation refocuses our souls for the business of the day. It is a way to reset our minds "on the things of the Spirit" and then "live according to the Spirit" (Rom. 8:5), which "is life and peace" (Rom. 8:6).

The mingling of meditation with memorization helps us obey the command of Colossians 3:2: "Set your minds on things that are above." It dials us in for the day with "spiritual truths to those who are spiritual," rather than walking as "the natural person" who "does not accept the things of the Spirit of God" (1 Cor. 2:13–14). And when we reset ourselves on the things of the Spirit by molding our minds with the words of God, the result is simply remarkable. Paul asks with Isaiah, "Who has understood *the mind of the Lord* so as to instruct him?" and answers with this stunning revelation: "we have *the mind of Christ*" (1 Cor. 2:16; see Isa. 40:13).

The Mind of Christ Is Yours

In other words, the apostle has two answers to the question, *Who has known the mind of the Lord?* The first is implied in the rhetorical question of Romans 11:34: "Who has known *the mind of the Lord*, or who has been his counselor?" Answer: no one. His mind is infinitely beyond ours. "How unsearchable are his judgments and how inscrutable are his ways!" (Rom. 11:33). No human may fully know the mind of God.

And yet Paul gives this second answer in 1 Corinthians 2:16: "we have *the mind of Christ*." As we not only read and study the Scriptures, but understand them, and then meditate on and memorize them, we increasingly "have the mind of Christ" as we are conformed to his image. We cannot know the mind of God exhaustively, but we can make real progress in degrees. And few ways, if any, imprint the mind of God on our minds like memorization, with meditation, of what he has so plainly said in the Scriptures.

Two Great Effects

One other text mentions "the mind of Christ" and points to two great effects of memorizing the mind of God. Philippians 2:5, as the introduction to the famous "Christ hymn" of Philippians 2:6–11, says, "Have this *mind* among yourselves, which is yours in Christ Jesus." And what will that mean in our lives? Two clear things in the immediate context are *unity* (Phil. 1:27–2:2) and *humility* (Phil. 2:3–4).

There is no better tuning fork for harmony in the body of Christ than the members striving together to conform their minds to the mind of Christ, not just with Christian concepts but with the very words of God. Having the mind of Christ will make us catalysts for a community "standing firm in one spirit, with *one mind* striving side by side for the faith of the gospel" (Phil. 1:27), and "being of *the same mind*, having the same love, being in full accord and of *one mind*" (Phil. 2:2).

And such "unity of mind" goes hand in hand with "a humble mind" in 1 Peter 3:8. Few things cultivate humility of mind like submitting our minds to the words of God by memorizing them. And so we become people ready to

> Do nothing from selfish ambition or conceit, but in humility count others more significant than yourselves. Let each of you look not only to his own interests, but also to the interests of others. (Phil. 2:3–4)

Hide God's words in your heart; build an arsenal for fighting temptation. But don't miss the life-changing power today of memorizing the mind of God.

———

Five Tips for Bible Memory

Some Scripture memory systems are amazingly involved. They can include boxes of memorized verses on cards, or long lists of previously memorized verses for review. I admire and appreciate those who have persevered in these systems and found them life-giving and sustainable in the long run. For me, such a process would threaten to dominate, if not devour, the limited time I realistically have on a daily basis for devotions.

Instead, I've found Scripture memory to be for me a tool in the belt of meditation, and one important pathway for Bible application. Meditation is the nonnegotiable habit of grace I want to practice each day, even if only briefly when life circumstances have crunched my time.[1] Scripture memory is not something, at least in every season of life, that I practice daily, but I aim on a weekly basis, if not a couple times each week, to spend several minutes seeking to memorize some powerful text I've come across in my Bible reading and want not only to meditate, but memorize, for my own soul or for the sake of ministry to others.

In regards to the latter, I once put together a list of "Ten Passages for Pastors to Memorize Cold," which are texts I've found especially helpful in ministering to others.[2] As for the former, for the feeding of your own soul, I've included on the following

---

[1] For more, see the afterword on communing with Christ on a "crazy day."
[2] Available online at desiringGod.org, July 10, 2013, http://www.desiringgod.org/blog/posts/ten-passages-for-pastors-to-memorize-cold.

pages "Ten Gospel Verses to Keep Warm," along with "Twelve Gospel Passages to Soak In."

Before providing those two short lists of gospel texts, here are five simple tips for Scripture memorization.

1. Diversify Your Picks

You can memorize whole books, or whole chapters (Romans 8 is a great starting point, or Philippians 3), or key sections.[3] My preference over the years has become key sections (say four to seven verses, like Titus 3:1–7) that I come across as I'm moving through a Bible-reading plan. It's often a section I find so densely rich that meditating on it for just a few minutes feels woefully inadequate. To enjoy more of its goodness, I need to put it to memory. (If you're looking to get started on a few key sections to memorize, try Col. 1:15–20; John 1:1–14; Heb. 1:1–4; and Phil. 2:5–11.)

2. Take It with You during the Day

Write the passage down or make it prominent and easily accessible on a tablet or phone. I wouldn't suggest quarantining your memorizing to a certain slot in the day, but unleash it into all of life. Play an audio recording in the car, look at a piece of paper while standing in line. Put a text on your home screen so you see it when you look at your smartphone.

3. Seek to Understand, Feel, and Apply the Text as You Memorize

Resist the urge to see simple memory as the goal. Learning the text "by heart" is secondary; taking the text *to heart* is primary.

---

[3] The most acclaimed text I know of for memorizing entire books of the Bible is Andrew Davis, *An Approach to Extended Memorization of Scripture*, available as an e-book as well as a free pdf online at http://www.fbcdurham.org/wp-content/uploads/2012/05/Scripture-Memory -Booklet-for-Publication-Website-Layout.pdf.

Don't memorize mindlessly, but engage the text and its meaning—not only its implications for your life, but what effects it should have on your emotions.

4. Turn Your Text into Prayer

Personal and corporate prayer times are a great time to exercise what you're memorizing, and see and feel it from a fresh angle as you turn it godward and express its significance for others. There have been times for me when praying some memorized text became the pathway for seeing fresh glories that had been hidden to me until then.

5. Memorize in Light of the Gospel

Finally, let the truth of Colossians 3:16 shape your memorization: "Let the word of Christ dwell in you richly." The "word of Christ" here, or "message of Christ," isn't first and foremost Scripture, but the gospel. So, in other words, memorize in light of the gospel.

Memorizing Scripture, in and of itself, isn't necessarily Christian. Jesus spoke with Jewish leaders who had memorized more of the Old Testament than we ever will, and he said to them, "You search the Scriptures because you think that in them you have eternal life; and it is they that bear witness about me, yet you refuse to come to me that you may have life" (John 5:39–40). And Paul spoke about Jews who intimately knew the Scriptures, but

> their minds were hardened. For to this day, when they read the old covenant, that same veil remains unlifted, because only through Christ is it taken away. Yes, to this day whenever Moses is read a veil lies over their hearts. But when one turns to the Lord, the veil is removed. (2 Cor. 3:14–16)

Whether we're memorizing texts from the Old Testament or the New, this is our need again and again: *to turn to the Lord.* In our memorizing, whether whole books or chapters or passages or single verses, we always must keep in mind Jesus's great lessons in Luke 24 about Bible interpretation: "He interpreted to them in all the Scriptures the things concerning himself" (Luke 24:27), and "he opened their minds to understand the Scriptures," and that "everything written about me in the Law of Moses and the Prophets and the Psalms must be fulfilled" (Luke 24:44–45).

Ten Gospel Verses to Keep Warm

Bible memorization is always time well spent. All Scripture memory is "profitable for teaching, for reproof, for correction, and for training in righteousness" (2 Tim. 3:16). And especially useful are one-verse statements of the gospel.

When you memorize a "gospel verse," and keep it warm, you have hidden in your heart a divinely inspired and inerrant expression, in human language, of the very point of the whole Bible and all of history. You carry with you the sword of the Spirit in its strongest alloy. One-sentence encapsulations of the Bible's central message strengthen our spiritual backbone and solidify our core, rooting us deep down in the bedrock of God's heart and the nature of the world he made, and sending us into confident combat with unbelief, whether our own or someone's else. Gospel verses are invaluable in both evangelism and discipleship.

So, alongside other Scripture memorization efforts, sprinkle in some gospel verses that guide and shape and flavor your whole reservoir. By "gospel verses," I have in mind verses like John 3:16 (don't begrudge this verse its fame—it's for good reason), verses that communicate succinctly that *Jesus saves sinners.*

Here's a starter list of ten. Perhaps keep your eyes peeled for others and add them as you go—and don't be surprised if you find a lot in Romans.

> The Son of Man came not to be served but to serve, and to give his life as a ransom for many. (Mark 10:45)

> God shows his love for us in that while we were still sinners, Christ died for us. (Rom. 5:8)

> The wages of sin is death, but the free gift of God is eternal life in Christ Jesus our Lord. (Rom. 6:23)

> There is therefore now no condemnation for those who are in Christ Jesus. (Rom. 8:1)

> He who did not spare his own Son but gave him up for us all, how will he not also with him graciously give us all things? (Rom. 8:32)

> For our sake he made him to be sin who knew no sin, so that in him we might become the righteousness of God. (2 Cor. 5:21)

> You know the grace of our Lord Jesus Christ, that though he was rich, yet for your sake he became poor, so that you by his poverty might become rich. (2 Cor. 8:9)

The saying is trustworthy and deserving of full acceptance, that Christ Jesus came into the world to save sinners, of whom I am the foremost. (1 Tim. 1:15)

In this is love, not that we have loved God but that he loved us and sent his Son to be the propitiation for our sins. (1 John 4:10)

Worthy are you to take the scroll
    and to open its seals,
for you were slain, and by your blood you ransomed
        people for God
    from every tribe and language and people and
        nation. (Rev. 5:9)

Twelve Gospel Passages to Soak In

Mere truth won't sustain our souls. We desperately need the gospel. "The grace of God in truth" (Col. 1:6) is the shock that brings a dead soul to life and the charge that keeps it living. The gospel is the fuel that awakens and energizes the human heart, not mere truth—essential as truth is. Two plus two equals four—that's true. It just doesn't do much to jump-start and drive a languishing soul.

It's all wonderful and good to learn various truths from the Bible—and there are many crucial truths to learn—but we must not miss or minimize the one truth of the gospel, "the word of the truth" (Col. 1:5; see Eph. 1:13), the message so central and significant that the apostle calls it not merely *a* truth, but *the* truth, throughout the Pastoral Epistles (1 Tim. 2:4; 3:15; 4:3; 6:5; 2 Tim. 2:18, 25; 3:7, 8; 4:4; Titus 1:1, 14).

In addition to the ten one-verse summaries of the gospel on the previous pages, here are twelve carefully selected "gospel passages" that get at the heart of the biblical good news in just two to four verses.

These short sections are ripe for memorization, and warrant at least some extended time of reflection. Build your life on them and around them, and let them shape and flavor everything. Soak in them—and soak them in.

> Surely he has borne our griefs
>   and carried our sorrows;
> yet we esteemed him stricken,
>   smitten by God, and afflicted.
> But he was pierced for our transgressions;
>   he was crushed for our iniquities;
> upon him was the chastisement that brought us peace,
>   and with his wounds we are healed.
> All we like sheep have gone astray;
>   we have turned—every one—to his own way;
> and the LORD has laid on him
>   the iniquity of us all. (Isa. 53:4–6)

> All have sinned and fall short of the glory of God, and are justified by his grace as a gift, through the redemption that is in Christ Jesus. (Rom. 3:23–24)

> Now to the one who works, his wages are not counted as a gift but as his due. And to the one who does not work but believes in him who justi-

fies the ungodly, his faith is counted as righteousness. (Rom. 4:4–5)

I delivered to you as of first importance what I also received: that Christ died for our sins in accordance with the Scriptures, that he was buried, that he was raised on the third day in accordance with the Scriptures. (1 Cor. 15:3–4)

Christ redeemed us from the curse of the law by becoming a curse for us—for it is written, "Cursed is everyone who is hanged on a tree"—so that in Christ Jesus the blessing of Abraham might come to the Gentiles, so that we might receive the promised Spirit through faith. (Gal. 3:13–14)

But God, being rich in mercy, because of the great love with which he loved us, even when we were dead in our trespasses, made us alive together with Christ—by grace you have been saved . . . (Eph. 2:4–5)

Though he was in the form of God, [Jesus] did not count equality with God a thing to be grasped, but emptied himself, by taking the form of a servant, being born in the likeness of men. And being found in human form, he humbled himself by becoming obedient to the point of death, even death on a cross. (Phil. 2:6–8)

In [Jesus] all the fullness of God was pleased to dwell, and through him to reconcile to himself all things, whether on earth or in heaven, making peace by the blood of his cross. (Col. 1:19–20)

You, who were dead in your trespasses and the uncircumcision of your flesh, God made alive together with him, having forgiven us all our trespasses, by canceling the record of debt that stood against us with its legal demands. This he set aside, nailing it to the cross. (Col. 2:13–14)

When the goodness and loving kindness of God our Savior appeared, he saved us, not because of works done by us in righteousness, but according to his own mercy, by the washing of regeneration and renewal of the Holy Spirit, whom he poured out on us richly through Jesus Christ our Savior, so that being justified by his grace we might become heirs according to the hope of eternal life. (Titus 3:4–7)

Since therefore the children share in flesh and blood, he himself likewise partook of the same things, that through death he might destroy the one who has the power of death, that is, the devil, and deliver all those who through fear of death were subject to lifelong slavery. For surely it is not angels that he helps, but he helps the offspring of Abraham. Therefore he had to be made like his brothers in every respect, so that he might become a merciful and faithful high priest in the service of God, to make propitiation for the sins of the people. (Heb. 2:14–17)

[Jesus] committed no sin, neither was deceit found in his mouth. When he was reviled, he did not revile in return; when he suffered, he did not threaten, but continued entrusting himself to him who judges justly. He himself bore our sins in his body on the tree, that we might die to sin and live to righteousness. By his wounds you have been healed. For you were straying like sheep, but have now returned to the Shepherd and Overseer of your souls. (1 Pet. 2:22–25)

Chapter 6

Resolve to Be a
Lifelong Learner

———

Wisdom does not come automatically with age. You'll find plenty of foolish old fogies out there. As Elihu declares in the book of Job, "It is the spirit in man, the breath of the Almighty, that makes him understand. It is not the old who are wise, nor the aged who understand what is right" (Job 32:8–9).

It is true that for many aged saints, gray hair and a good head go hand in hand. But for others, far too many others, length of life only entrenches stubbornness, irritability, and careless ways of thinking and living. Life experience may increase inevitably with age, but without some long-term pattern of receptivity and intentionality, multiplied experiences will only create more confusion than clarity.

For Christians in particular, the stakes are even higher for cultivating holy curiosity and the mind-set of a lifelong learner. Teaching and learning are at the heart of our faith. To be a "disciple" means literally to be a "learner." Our Master is the consummate teacher, and the central task of his undershepherds in the local church is teaching (Matt. 28:20; 1 Tim. 3:2; 5:17; Titus 1:9; Heb. 13:7). God designed the church to be a community of lifelong learners under the earthly guidance of leaders who are teachers at heart.

The Christian faith is not a finite course of study for the front-end of adulthood. Our mind-set shouldn't be to first do our learning and then spend the rest of our lives drawing from that original deposit of knowledge. Rather, ongoing health in the Christian life is inextricably linked to ongoing learning.

Learning Till the Day of Christ—and Beyond

Many of us have felt the comforting balm of Philippians 1:6, that "he who began a good work in you will bring it to completion. . . ." But the statement doesn't end there. Yes, we have the great promise of his completing his work in us, but then follows a sobering disclosure about the timing: "at the day of Jesus Christ." The loop of learning doesn't close today or tomorrow, but as Jesus tarries, a lifetime lies ahead.

And even in heaven, and then in the new creation, we shouldn't expect that our learning will be done. In our Beloved, we have a bounty of blessings such that "in the coming ages [God will] show the immeasurable riches of his grace in kindness toward us in Christ Jesus" (Eph. 2:7). We're not given them all at once, but forever we have new mercies to receive, fresh revelations to discover, new things to learn about our Lord. We are given a promise of increase that is not only lifelong, but eternal.

And so we are lifelong learners, to say the least. Two important questions then lie before us in this short chapter: a simple *what* and a simple *how*. One, what is the framework for our lifelong learning? Is there a grid or focus or organizing principle as we continue to learn and grow? And two, how might we go about practicing such learning for a lifetime?

Center on the Word

There is indeed something we frontload for the Christian life, and then spend the rest of our days exploring and going deeper in: it is the "word" or "message" about Jesus, God's incarnate Word. Simply put, the focal point and center of our lifelong learning is the person and work of Christ. All things are in him, through him, and for him (Col. 1:17).

When we say "learners," we don't mean of mere facts, information, and head knowledge. We mean all that *and more*. We don't just learn facts, but we learn a Face. We're not just learners of principles, but of a Person. We are lifelong learners in relationship with Jesus as we hear his voice in his word and have his ear in prayer, and share in community with his body, all through the power of his Spirit.

And one of the chief ways we know his person more is by learning more about his work for us. Not only are we "rooted and grounded" in Christ's love for us at Calvary, but we press on "to comprehend with all the saints what is the breadth and length and height and depth, and to know the love of Christ that surpasses knowledge, that [we] may be filled with all the fullness of God" (Eph. 3:17–19).

The heart of lifelong learning that is truly *Christian* is not merely digging deeper in the seemingly bottomless store of information there is to learn about the world and humanity and history, but plunging into the infinite flood of Christ's love, and how it all comes back to this, in its boundless breadth and length and height and depth, and seeing everything else in its light. The center of lifelong learning for the Christian is this: knowing and enjoying God himself in Christ through the gospel word and the written word of the Scriptures—in the hearing and reading and study and meditation and memorization of the Bible. And so we include this chapter on lifelong learning here in part 1 on hearing God's voice.

Five Principles for Lifelong Learning

The *what*, then, is "the Word"—incarnate, spoken, and written—at the center, casting its long shadow on all other learning. But now, *how*? The short answer is that the list of particular practices for lifelong learning can be as diverse as creativity will allow. Do your own brainstorming here. And find fresh ways as you go. The following are five big-picture suggestions to get you going on cultivating habits for lifelong learning.

1. VARY YOUR SOURCES AND SEASONS

Learn from personal conversations, read books, take classes, watch educational videos, and (perhaps most underrated) listen to recorded audio. Diversify your sources of teaching.

- Personal conversations with experienced and knowledgeable people are tops on the list, as you can dialogue and ask questions and receive words of wisdom tailored just for you, as they're aware of your situation and needs.
- Books have the value of being accessible anytime and anywhere; you can go at your speed, in your time and place, and reread as needed.
- Classes provide the advantage of learning in context with others, benefiting from their questions, and being forced to focus on the material at some set time for some particular season.
- Educational videos provide the flexibility of watching at a time most convenient to you and the benefit from visuals (diagrams, charts, body language, facial expressions).
- Listening to recordings gives the flexibility for multitasking (learning while driving or exercising or cleaning) and en-

gages the mind in ways different from video instruction by leaning on the imagination to picture the teacher and setting.

Also, consider how the sources will change in your various seasons of life. College and seminary are concentrated seasons for classroom instruction, educational dialogue, and extended reading. If you have a long commute, or the kind of manual-labor job that permits it, you can take advantage of audio books and courses and lectures and sermons. Evaluate the particulars of your season of life and choose the media and venues most conducive to your ongoing learning about God, the world, and yourself.

2. Create Space and Redeem Spare Time

If you work a full-time job and have a young family, it may be difficult to make room for the homework and the weekly commitment of attending an evening class or even taking a course online. But what you can do, in this tight season or any other, is create little windows for learning.

It may be only five or ten minutes of reading as you go to bed at night, or a few extra minutes of lingering over the Scriptures in the morning, or listening to a short podcast like *Ask Pastor John* as you brush your teeth, commute, or run errands.[1] Or maybe set a goal to read an article or two each day online at a substantive site like The Gospel Coalition.[2] Or try to content yourself with keeping a bookmark in a print book or on an electronic reader as you work through a good book just a few minutes at a time.

3. Mind Your Mindless Moments

There's a place for mental rest and recreation, for ball games and television and pop tunes and motion pictures, but a lifelong

---

[1] http://www.desiringgod.org/AskPastorJohn/.
[2] http://www.thegospelcoalition.org/.

learner will want to take care that most of life's spare moments are not cannibalized by mere mindless entertainment. There is a way to watch sports and television to the glory of God, and with intentionality for learning. Checking on the news is one. The *History* channel or some good documentary are among others.

Lifelong learning, over time, will mean developing the resistance to simply veg out whenever you feel the impulse, and rather to turn some of these moments, if not many, into opportunities to grow. It may not feel like much on any given day, but the payoff over the long haul is enormous.

4. Adapt to New Media

A large personal library, with tattered and penciled pages, was once the mark of a lifelong learner. Then the shelves of books were accompanied by newspaper and magazine clippings, then stacks of 8-track tapes, then stashes of cassettes, then piles of CDs. Today a veritable library can be stored on an e-reader or laptop, and MP3s once hoarded on hard drives are available online through near ubiquitous Wi-Fi.

Podcasts have become a favorite channel of the endlessly curious, and tomorrow the technology will be new and even better. Already free video and online education courses are accessible like never before. And there is social media—and what teachers or entertainers or athletes or friends you let fill your feed says a lot about how eager you are to simply kill a few moments scrolling or bring them to life with learning.

5. Embrace the Identity of Learner

Finally, given the importance of regular teaching and lifelong learning in healthy Christianity, begin to consider yourself a learner. Claim it as your sixth strength. Fight against the tide that takes learning to be something quarantined to school days and essential to childhood and adolescence but something beneath adulthood. Resist the urge to squander spare time on mindless entertainment without limit. Embrace your finitude and the glorious infinity of God, and brace yourself to never stop learning, not as a burden, but a great joy. Own the truth that in a sense we creatures never "arrive," not even in the new creation.

Resolve to be a lifelong learner.

Part 2

HAVE HIS EAR

Prayer

Chapter 7

Enjoy the Gift of Having God's Ear

He is "the God of all grace" (1 Pet. 5:10). Not only did he choose us before the world began, and give his Son to save us, and cause us to be born again, but he also sustains the whole of our Christian lives, from day one to that Day, in his matchless grace. He covers our lives with his unexpected kindness through people and circumstances, in good times and bad, and showers us with unforeseen favor in sickness and health, in life and in death.

But as we've seen, he doesn't always catch us off guard. Or even usually. God has his regular channels—the means of grace—those well-worn pathways along which he is so often pleased to pass and pour out his goodness on those waiting expectantly. The chief thoroughfares are his word, his church, and prayer. Or his voice, his body, and his ear. Now we turn from our focus on his voice to his ear.

But we must see his listening to us in prayer in relation to our listening to him in his word.

The Speaking God Who Listens

First sounds his voice. By his word, he reveals himself and expresses his heart, and unveils his Son as the culmination of his speaking. By his word, he creates (Gen. 1:3) and re-creates (2 Cor. 4:4), not just individual members, but a body called the church (which is the means of grace we'll turn to in part 3).

And wonder of wonders, not only does he express himself and bid us hear his voice, but he wants to hear ours. The speaking God not only has spoken, but he also listens—he stops, he stoops, he wants to hear from you. He stands ready to hear your voice.

Christian, you have the ear of God. We call it prayer.

A Conversation We Didn't Start

Prayer, simply put, is talking to God. It is irreducibly relational. It's personal—he is the Absolute Person, and we are derivative persons, fashioned in his image. In a sense, prayer is as basic as persons relating to each other, conversing, interacting, but with this significant caveat: in this relationship, we don't chat as peers. He is Creator, and we are creatures. He is the great Lord, and we are his happy servants. Yet because of his amazing love and extravagant grace, he invites us to interact. He has opened his mouth and spoken to us. Now he opens his ear to hear us.

Prayer, for the Christian, is not merely talking to God, but responding to the One who has initiated toward us. He has spoken first. This is not a conversation we start, but a relationship into which we've been drawn. His voice breaks the silence. Then, in prayer, we speak to the God who has spoken. Our asking and pleading and requesting originate not from our emptiness, but his fullness. Prayer doesn't begin with our needs, but with his bounty. Its origin is first in adoration, and only later in asking. Prayer is a reflex to the grace he gives to the sinners he saves. It is soliciting his provision in view of the power he has shown.

Prayer is the glad response from the bride, in a joyfully submissive relationship with her Groom, responding to his sacrificial and life-giving initiatives. And so it is stunning grace we find in such a simple statement from the psalmist, which applies to every Christian, "The LORD accepts my prayer" (Ps. 6:9).

The Great Purpose of Prayer

It shouldn't surprise us, then, to find that prayer is not finally about getting things from God, but getting God. Born in response to his voice, prayer makes its requests of God, but is not content to only receive from God. Prayer must have him. John Piper writes,

> It is not wrong to want God's gifts and ask for them. Most prayers in the Bible are for the gifts of God. But ultimately every gift should be desired because it shows us and brings us more of him. . . . When this world totally fails, the ground for joy remains. God. Therefore, surely every prayer for life and health and home and family and job and ministry in this world is secondary. And the great purpose of prayer is to ask that—in and through all his gifts—God would be our joy.[1]

Or, as C. S. Lewis so memorably said, "Prayer in the sense of petition, asking for things, is a small part of it; confession and penitence are its threshold, adoration its sanctuary, the presence and vision and enjoyment of God its bread and wine."[2] The great purpose of prayer is to come humbly, expectantly, and—because of Jesus—boldly into the conscious presence of God, to relate to him, talk with him, and ultimately enjoy him as our great Treasure.

---

[1] *When I Don't Desire God: How to Fight for Joy* (Wheaton, IL: Crossway, 2004), 142–43.
[2] *The World's Last Night and Other Essays* (New York: Mariner Books, 2002), 8.

Prayer's Practices in Perspective

So, prayer—having God's ear—is ultimately about having more of God. And having God's ear (like hearing his voice) is not first and foremost about our particular practices and postures—the specific habits we develop—but the principle of continually relating to him, privately and with others. He is holy, and so we worship (adoration). He is merciful, and so we repent (confession). He is gracious, and so we express appreciation (thanksgiving). He is loving and caring, and so we petition him for ourselves, our family, our friends, and our world (supplication).[3]

Because prayer is part and parcel of an ongoing relationship with God, the book of Acts doesn't accent the particular times and places of early-church prayer, but tells us, "All these with one accord were *devoting themselves to prayer*" (Acts 1:14). And Paul charges the church not to specific prescribed habits, but to "be constant in prayer" (Rom. 12:12), to "continue steadfastly in prayer" (Col. 4:2), to "pray without ceasing" (1 Thess. 5:17), to be "praying at all times in the Spirit, with all prayer and supplication" (Eph. 6:18). Prayer is first and foremost an orientation of life, rather than the particular practices and patterns which might be characteristic of a certain community or season of life, or season of church history.

Such a pervasive call to prayer as we see in the New Testament is not the stuff of impersonal achievement and raw discipline, but intimate relationship. It has underneath it not an iron human will, but an extraordinarily attentive divine Father who is eager to "give good things to those who ask him" (Matt. 7:11). Not only is he a Father who reveals his bounty in words, and "knows what you need before you ask him" (Matt. 6:8),

---

[3] Adoration (A), confession (C), thanksgiving (T), and supplication (S) form the memorable ACTS of prayer, which is a simple mnemonic device for the various kinds of prayer that make our approach to God healthy and whole. We'll say more in the next chapter about the ACTS of prayer.

but he wants you to ask. He wants to hear. He wants to interact. He means to have us not in a hypothetical relationship, but in reality. He is even more ready to hear us than we are to pray.

In Jesus's Name We Pray

All this is possible only through the person and work of God's Son. Not only did Jesus die for our sins (1 Cor. 15:3), to show God's love for us (Rom. 5:8), but he rose from the grave and ascended to heaven as "a forerunner on our behalf" (Heb. 6:20), appearing in the very presence of the Father (Heb. 9:24). Jesus is "at the right hand of God, who indeed is interceding for us" (Rom. 8:34). Having conquered death, the God-man, stationed in his glorified body, "is able to save to the uttermost those who draw near to God through him, since he always lives to make intercession for them" (Heb. 7:25). Our having God's ear is as sure as our having God's Son.

And so in this light, we turn general intentions into more specific pathways in the coming chapters, and then into even more specific plans in our particular communities and individual lives. We develop habits of life—habits of grace. We find a regular time and place. We pray by ourselves and with others. We pray "in the closet" and throughout the day. Prayer is scheduled and spontaneous. It's in the car, at the table, in between appointments, and beside the bed. We pray through Scripture, in direct response to God's word. We adore, confess, give thanks, and ask. We learn to pray by praying, and by praying with others, and discover that "praying regularly with others can be one of the most enriching adventures of your Christian life."[4] We will explore all that and more in the pages to come.

We have the ear of God. Let's make the most of this.

---

[4] Donald S. Whitney, *Spiritual Disciplines for the Christian Life*, rev. ed. (Colorado Springs: NavPress, 2014), 93.

Chapter 8

Pray in Secret

———

Now is the time to take a fresh look at your private prayer life. Perhaps you'll find a tweak or two that you could make in the coming days. Typically the best way to grow and make headway is not a total overhaul, but identifying one or a couple small changes that will pay dividends over time.

Or maybe you have little-to-no real private prayer life (which might be as common today among professing Christians as it's ever been), and you really need to start from scratch. You may feel first-hand the weight of Francis Chan's alarm: "My biggest concern for this generation is your inability to focus, especially in prayer."[1] Perhaps it's true of you, and you're ready for change.

Whether you're in need of a little self-evaluation or learning as a beginner, I'd like to offer a few practical pointers on private prayer. But let's start with why private prayer, or "closet prayer," is so important in the first place.

---

[1] Spoken from the stage at Passion 2015 in Atlanta, January 3, 2015.

Praying "in the Closet"

"Closet prayer" gets its name from Jesus's famous Sermon on the Mount in Matthew 5–8. The context is Jesus's instructions for not "practicing your righteousness before other people in order to be seen by them" (Matt. 6:1).

> When you pray, you must not be like the hypocrites. For they love to stand and pray in the synagogues and at the street corners, that they may be seen by others. Truly, I say to you, they have received their reward. But when you pray, go into your room and shut the door and pray to your Father who is in secret. And your Father who sees in secret will reward you. (Matt. 6:5–6)

Just as praying in earshot of others had its immanent rewards in first-century Judaism, so also it does in our twenty-first-century church communities, whether it's in church or small group or just at the table with friends and family. It can be easy to slide into impressing others as the driving motivation for our praying with others, whether it's our length, tone, topic, mood, or word choice, all carefully chosen to produce certain effects in our human hearers alone.

It's a tough line to walk, because we must pray with others—in church and in our homes and elsewhere—and public prayer *should* take into account that others are listening; it *should* have others in mind. But the danger lurks of sidelining God and shifting our focus to making ourselves look impressive.

But "closet prayer" offers a test of authenticity for our public praying. As Tim Keller comments on Matthew 6:5–6:

> The infallible test of spiritual integrity, Jesus says, is your private prayer life. Many people will pray when they are required by cultural or social expectations, or perhaps by

the anxiety caused by troubling circumstances. Those with a genuinely lived relationship with God as Father, however, will inwardly *want* to pray and therefore will pray even though nothing on the outside is pressing them to do so. They pursue it even during times of spiritual dryness, when there is no social or experiential payoff.[2]

Private prayer is an important test of whether we are real. Is he our true treasure, or are we simply using prayer to appear godly and impress others? Are our prayers really directed toward a God who hears us and wants to do us good, or is prayer a tool for our getting what we want from others? Private prayer cuts through the fog and confusion and helps to show that our relationship with God is authentic.

Remedy for Inadequacy

But private prayer is not just a test of our trueness, but also an ongoing remedy for our inadequacies and the lack of desire we often feel for God. Prayer, says John Piper, is "not only the measure of our hearts, revealing what we really desire, it is also the indispensible remedy for our hearts when we do not desire God the way we ought."[3]

Private prayer shows who we really are spiritually *and* is essential in healing the many places we find ourselves broken, needy, lacking, and rebellious.

Context for Relationship

Also, as Keller notes, prayer is essential for "a genuinely lived relationship with God as Father."[4] This is the heart of prayer—not getting things from God, but getting God. Prayer is where

---

[2] *Prayer: Experiencing Awe and Intimacy with God* (New York: Dutton, 2014), 23.

[3] *When I Don't Desire God: How to Fight for Joy* (Wheaton, IL: Crossway, 2004), 153.

[4] Keller, *Prayer*, 23.

we speak back to God, in response to his word to us, and experience what it means to enjoy him as an end in himself, not just a means to our petitions. In prayer, we enjoy the gift of having God's ear (chap. 7) and discover for ourselves that we are not just servants, but friends (John 15:15). We are not just hearers of his word, but his own children who have his heart (Rom. 8:15–16; Gal. 4:6–7). He wants to hear from us. Such is the power and privilege of prayer.

Here's where we see why Jesus practiced so well what he preached about prayer and finding a "closet." He had no inadequacies to make up for, and no doubts about his trueness, but he desperately desired fellowship with his Father. And so, again and again, he prayed alone. "After he had dismissed the crowds, he went up on the mountain by himself to pray. . . . He was there alone" (Matt. 14:23; also Mark 6:46). Not just once, but as a regular habit, he "would withdraw to desolate places and pray" (Luke 5:16). "Rising very early in the morning, while it was still dark, he departed and went out to a desolate place, and there he prayed" (Mark 1:35).

Before selecting his twelve disciples, "he went out to the mountain to pray, and all night he continued in prayer to God" (Luke 6:12). Even in Gethsemane, three times he "went away and prayed" (Matt. 26:36, 42, 44; also Mark 14:32–42). From the beginning of his ministry to the eve of his crucifixion, he made the practice of private prayer an essential part of his relationship with the Father.

And so, it is difficult to overstate the place of private prayer. It is, in many ways, the measure of who we are spiritually. How we pray, says J. I. Packer, "is as important a question as we can ever face."[5]

---

[5] *My Path of Prayer: Personal Glimpses of the Glory and the Majesty of God Revealed through Experiences of Prayer*, ed. David Hanes (West Sussex, UK: Henry Walter, 1981), 56.

Five Suggestions for Secret Prayer

That private prayer is important, even essential, for the Christian is clear. But how we go about private prayer is gloriously open for our various experiences and routines and patterns, in the differing seasons of our lives. As you evaluate (or begin) your own rhythms and habits, here are five suggestions for enriching private prayer.

1. CREATE YOUR CLOSET

Find your regular place for private prayer, and if you can't locate a ready-made spot, make one. It may simply be a clean desk, or someplace you can kneel. Many of us have found that beside the bed proves more fruitful than lying in bed. Maybe you can find an actual closet, or nook under the stairs, with enough space to sit or kneel, and enough light to read and even capture notes. It will help you be regular in private prayer to have your go-to spot.

2. BEGIN WITH BIBLE

Because prayer is a conversation we didn't start, but a response to God's initiation and speaking to us in his word, many of us have learned, with George Mueller, to start with the Scriptures. Mueller says that for ten years, he began each day with an immediate attempt at fervent and extended prayer, only to eventually learn how much richer and focused his prayers were when they came in response to God's word.

From then on, Mueller began with a brief prayer for God's help as he read, then he went first to the Bible and would open his ear to God in his word by meditating on the Scriptures, then transition, through the discipline of meditation (chap. 3), into his season of daily private prayer.[6]

---

[6] *A Narrative of Some of the Lord's Dealings with George Mueller, Written by Himself, Jehovah Magnified. Addresses by George Mueller Complete and Unabridged*, 2 vols. (Muskegon, MI: Dust and Ashes, 2003), 1:272–73. For an excellent new book on this topic, see Donald S. Whitney, *Praying the Bible* (Wheaton, IL: Crossway, 2015).

3. ADORE, CONFESS, THANK, ASK

After reading and meditating on the Bible, and before opening the gates to "free prayer"—voicing whatever is on our hearts—it can help to have some form ready at hand. William Law counseled that morning devotions "have something fixed and something at liberty."[7] So also with private prayer.

Martin Luther recommended praying through the form of the Lord's Prayer with fresh wording each day. One time-tested form is ACTS: adoration, confession, thanksgiving, supplication. First, *adore* God with praise for the truth revealed in your reading of and meditation on the Scriptures, then *confess* your own sins and failings and foibles, then *give thanks* for his grace and mercy, and finally *supplicate*—petition him, ask him—for requests for yourself, your family, your church, and beyond.

4. DIVULGE YOUR DESIRES — AND DEVELOP THEM

First, something fixed; now, something at liberty. This is "free prayer," where we pray our hearts, and what burdens and anxieties are on us that day and in that season of life. In private prayer, we are our most honest with God and with ourselves. Express your heart to your Father. He knows it already, and he wants to hear it from you. This is an unspeakable privilege.

But prayer to God is not only the place for divulging our heart, but also developing our desires. There is power here. Prayer changes our hearts like nothing else—perhaps especially when we follow the prayers of the Bible, in the psalms and from the apostle (as in Eph. 1:17–21; 3:16–19; Phil. 1:9–11; Col. 1:9–12), as guides for the shaping and expressing of our desires toward God.

---

[7] Law, *A Serious Call to a Devout and Holy Life* (Grand Rapids, MI: Eerdmans, 1966), 154.

5. Keep It Fresh

Change it up for a new year, or a new month, or a new season of life. Regularly, or just on occasion, write out prayers with focus and care (this is a valuable facet of the discipline of journaling, as we'll see in chap. 11), or sharpen your affections in prayer with fasting (chap. 10), or take a break from the chaos of life with some special retreat for silence and solitude (chap. 12).

Few things are as worthy of your attention and investment as the privilege and power of private prayer.

———

The habits of regular private prayer will change in various seasons of life. There have been seasons in which I've kept bulleted lists to pray through daily, or items to pray through weekly. I've kept detailed notes about what I was praying for on particular days, and tried to circle back to make notes about answered prayers or altered desires. Another helpful practice has been writing out or typing daily prayers (more on this in chap. 11 on journaling).

In recent years, I've found it most helpful to pray just briefly at the outset of my devotional time something like, "Father, please bless the reading of your words to my heart this morning," trying to keep it fresh each day. Then after reading, and hopefully meditating on some section from the reading, I try to transition into prayer based on what I've been meditating, using the rough pattern of adoration, confession, thanksgiving, supplication (the well-known ACTS of prayer).

I typically begin with praise or "adoration," speaking words of worship to God for who he is, what he's done for me, or what he promises to do in light of the text on which I've meditated. I hope to linger here, at least for several sentences, cultivating a heart of worship as I dig to put into words the glory I've glimpsed in his word.

Next is confession. Still in view of my moments of meditation, I'll confess my sins and inadequacies and failures, both general and specific, depending on the truth in view.

Next, I seek to cultivate gratitude toward God as I express words of thanksgiving for his grace and mercy, that despite his grandeur and my smallness, his holiness and my sinfulness, he has rescued me and made me his own in Jesus.

Finally, I turn to supplication, to specific requests for myself and those I love, first flowing from the truth in view during meditation and then letting it broaden out to what's on my mind and schedule for the day. Presently, my seasons of prayer have been almost exclusively meditation-driven, and guided by what's on my mind and heart that day, rather than list-driven.[8]

Private prayer can be an intensely personal time between you and God. It should be. As you make a regular practice of hearing God's voice, and responding to him in prayer, you will develop your own habits of grace for enjoying God in prayer.

---

[8] I don't disparage the keeping and praying of lists, but would caution you to avoid the dangers outlined by Timothy Keller, citing J. I. Packer. *Prayer: Experiencing Awe and Intimacy with God* (New York: Dutton, 2014), 229–30.

Chapter 9

Pray with Constancy and Company

As we've seen, prayer is at the very heart of the Christian life. Not only is it obedience to God's command, but it is a vital means of our receiving his ongoing grace for our spiritual survival and thriving. And the joy of prayer—communing with God—is essential to what it means to be Christian. Without prayer, there is no true relationship with him, and no deep delight in who he is, but only glimpses from afar.

As Jesus teaches, private prayer (or "closet prayer") has an important role to play in the life of the believer. We develop our various patterns and practices for secret prayer in the rhythms of our unique lives. We find our place and time to "go into your room and shut the door and pray to your Father who is in secret" (Matt. 6:6). Amen to private prayer (chap. 8). It is crucial. But there is more.

Taking Prayer into the Day

Prayer begins in secret, but God doesn't mean for it to stay in the closet. Prayer is for all of life, and especially for our life together in community. When we follow the lead of the Scriptures, we not only practice prayer in private, but take its spirit of dependence and trust into the rest of the day, and into times of focused prayer together with fellow believers.

Likely you know the verses that lead us to whisper prayers long after we've left the closet. "Pray without ceasing" (1 Thess. 5:17); "be constant in prayer" (Rom. 12:12); "continue steadfastly in prayer" (Col. 4:2); "pray at all times" (Eph. 6:18). Jesus said that we "ought always to pray and not lose heart" (Luke 18:1). These texts charge us not to stay all day in the closet, but to carry a posture of prayer in the soul as we give ourselves fully to our daily tasks and engagements—and that in a moment, we be ready to go consciously godward in the car, waiting in line, as we walk, before a meal, in the midst of a difficult conversation, and in anything else.

"Everywhere God is, prayer is," Tim Keller writes. "Since God is everywhere and infinitely great, prayer must be all-pervasive in our lives."[1]

The High Point: Praying Together

The high point of all-pervasive prayer, outside the closet door, is praying together with other Christians. Arranging for accompaniment in prayer takes more energy than a whispered prayer while on the move. It takes planning and initiative and the syncing of schedules in a way that private prayer does not. But it is worth every ounce of effort.

And so we have at least two fronts to a healthy life of prayer. We pray personally, in secret and on the move, and we pray corporately, resisting the privatizing of our prayers, not just by asking others to pray for us but especially by having others pray *with* us.

---

[1] *Prayer: Experiencing Awe and Intimacy with God* (New York: Dutton, 2014), 28.

Christ and His Company

If any human life would have been fine without regular company in prayer, it would have been Jesus's. But again and again we catch glimpses of a life of prayer that was not only personal but corporate. "He took with him Peter and John and James and went up on the mountain to pray" (Luke 9:28), and he responded gladly to their inquiry, "Lord, teach us to pray" (Luke 11:1), with a communal prayer to "*our* Father," marked by the repeated use of "we," "us," and "our."

The classic text on Jesus's letting others invade his prayer space is Luke 9:18: "Now it happened that as he was praying alone, the disciples were with him." Rarely did he part company with his men (and only then to pray, see Matt. 14:23; Mark 1:35; Luke 5:16), and doubtless one of their regular pursuits together was prayer. Keeping such company in prayer must have played a part in "the boldness of Peter and John [who were] uneducated, common men," when it was recognized "that they had been with Jesus" (Acts 4:13).

Jesus's communal prayer with his men then led to communal prayer in the early church they led. It is explicit at nearly every turn in the book of Acts.

- "All these with one accord were devoting themselves to prayer" (1:14; also 2:42).
- "They lifted their voices together to God" (4:24), and the filling of the Holy Spirit fell after they prayed together (v. 31).
- The church chose the seven, and "they prayed and laid their hands on them" (6:6).
- While Peter was in prison, "earnest prayer for him was made to God by the church" (12:5), and when he escaped miraculously, he found "many were gathered together and were praying" (v. 12).
- It was "after fasting and praying" that the church in Antioch sent Paul and Barnabas out on the first missionary

journey (13:3), and "when they had appointed elders for them in every church, with prayer and fasting they committed them to the Lord" (14:23).

- Even in jail, "Paul and Silas were praying and singing hymns to God" (16:25).
- And in an emotional goodbye to the Ephesian elders, Paul "knelt down and prayed with them all" (20:36; also 21:5).

Five Counsels for Praying with Company

Our need for God's help today is no less than the early church's, and prayer *together* remains a vital means of God's ongoing grace in the Christian life and for our communities.

That the early church prayed together is plain; the details of how they went about it are not. This is significant. There is no one pattern for corporate prayer, whether it's in twos or tens, hundreds or thousands. The practices of praying together vary from family to family, church to church, and community to community based on context, leadership, and shared history. Wise leaders are observant of what habits and practices are already at work in the group, which ones are helpful and could be encouraged, and which ones might prove unhelpful over the long haul and could be replaced.

Here are five lessons I've learned in leading small-group prayer in recent years. Maybe one or two would be good for a family, community group, or church you lead or are a part of.

1. Make It Regular

Make regular prayer with company a part of your weekly or biweekly routine. Instead of just hit-or-miss, have a planned time and place to gather with fellow believers to pray. As for how many weeks or months you commit, make a finite pledge together, rather than a world-without-end-amen kind of plan. When the specified time is up, renew or reconsider. Regular prayer commitments without an end date tend to fizzle over time, and then prove discouraging for future engagements.

2. Start with Scripture

Christian prayer at its truest comes in response to God's self-revelation to us. It is, as George Herbert wrote, "God's breath in man returning to his birth."[2] And so it is fitting to begin sessions of corporate prayer with some anchor in God's own speaking to us by reading a passage or referencing some place in Scripture as a kind of "call to prayer." We inhale the Scriptures and exhale in prayer.

3. Limit Share Time

It can be easy to let the sharing of requests cannibalize the actual praying together. Keep your introductions short, read a passage, and go right into prayer. Encourage people to share their requests by praying them with the information needed to let others in on what they're praying.

4. Encourage Brevity and Focus

The corporate setting is not well served by rambling. It tries the attention and focus of even the most devout prayer warriors, and contributes to setting a length standard inaccessible to many and a poor model to everyone. At suitable times, urge short, focused prayers, and perhaps even include an explicit season of one-sentence praises or thanks which can encourage more people to participate.

5. Pray without Show, but with Others in Mind

Remind yourself that corporate prayer is not for impressing others—some personalities especially need the regular prompt—

---

[2] "Prayer (I)," available online at Poetry Foundation, http://www.poetryfoundation.org/poem/173636.

but for gathering others up with us in our praises, confessions, thanksgivings, and requests. However, minding our own penchant for praying for show doesn't mean we forget or neglect the others gathered.

Good corporate praying is not directed just to God, but has our fellow pray-ers in view. This means that, like Jesus, we pray most often with "we," "us," and "our," and with both authenticity and candor that is appropriate for those assembled.

———

Nine Profits of Praying with Company

It is almost too good to be true—almost—that in Jesus we have the very ear of God. What an indescribable gift that the God whose greatness is beyond comprehension actually stoops to listen to us.

But the joys and benefits of prayer aren't limited to our personal prayer lives. A shared joy is a doubled joy, and as we've seen, God means for us not only to pray in our closets, and "without ceasing" (1 Thess. 5:17) as we move through life in a spirit of dependence, but to pray with company.

Inestimable good happens, no doubt, when the regenerate rally with their fellows; it is past finding out all that God is doing when we pray together. Yet it helps to trace out some of the good, and whet our appetites for some of the graces for which our prayer together is a means. So in helping us celebrate the place and power of corporate prayer, here are nine profits of praying with company.

1. For Added Power

Matthew 18:15–20 may be one of the more misunderstood texts in the New Testament. That often quoted promise "where two or three are gathered in my name, there am I among them" (v. 20) comes at the end of a section on church discipline and when a "brother sins against you" (v. 15). However, Jesus does appeal to a deeper principle here, which is a benefit of corporate prayer. He says, "If two of you agree on earth about *anything* they ask . . ." (v. 19). There is an added power to our prayers when we unite with fellows in the faith and make our requests to the Father with our hearts joined together.

2. For Multiplied Joy

Let's make explicit what we said above: When we share the joy of prayer, we double our joy. When we make the regular practice of praying together with fellow believers, we avail ourselves of a channel of joy we otherwise would be neglecting. And by praying with others, we not only add to our joy, but also to theirs. And when we work with others for their joy in God (2 Cor. 1:24), we again increase our own.

3. For Greater Glory to God

Our multiplied joy in God then makes for multiplied glory to God—because *God is most glorified in us when we are most satisfied in him.*[3] If we hear gratitude to him in terms of God's glory—which we should in light of Romans 1:21, where giving thanks to him is connected to honoring him as God—then 2 Corinthians 1:11 makes this truth explicit as it relates to prayer: "You also must help us by prayer, so that many will give thanks on our behalf for the blessing granted us through the prayers of many." Praying together not only adds power to the request, but also means more glory for the Giver when he answers.

---

[3] This is the refrain of John Piper throughout his corpus, and the mission of desiringGod.org, which I serve as executive editor, is to help people everywhere understand and embrace this truth.

4. FOR FRUITFUL MINISTRY AND MISSION

God means for us to pray for each other in our various ministries and manifestations of mission, in light of our great shared Commission. Paul modeled this in asking the churches to pray for his gospel work (Rom. 15:30–32; 2 Cor. 1:11; Eph. 6:18–20; Col. 4:3–4; 2 Thess. 3:1). He was more than able to pray these things himself, and doubtless he did. But he anticipated there would be greater fruitfulness in the work when others joined him in prayer for it.

5. FOR UNITY AMONG BELIEVERS

Praying together is one of the single most significant things we can do together to cultivate unity in the church. There is a unity that is a given to those who are fellows in Christ and share spiritual life in him. Acts 1:14 says it was "with one accord" that the first Christians "were devoting themselves to prayer." Already we have "the unity of the Spirit," and yet we are to be "eager to maintain" it (Eph. 4:3). So praying together is both an effect of the unity we already share in Christ and a cause for deeper and richer unity. It's not only a sign that unity exists among the brothers but also a catalyst for more.

6. FOR ANSWERS WE OTHERWISE WOULDN'T GET

James 5:14–16 implies that there are some answers to prayer we simply would not get without involving others in our praying.

> Is anyone among you sick? Let him call for the elders of the church, and let them pray over him, anointing him with oil in the name of the Lord.[4] And the prayer of faith will save

---

[4] Much could be said about the act of anointing with oil. While this is not the place for a full treatment, it is worth briefly summarizing, in a book on the means of grace, the essence of this act and how it can accompany prayer as a means of grace for the Christian.

the one who is sick, and the Lord will raise him up. And if he has committed sins, he will be forgiven. Therefore, confess your sins to one another and pray for one another, that you may be healed. The prayer of a righteous person has great power as it is working.

God means for some answers to prayer to await the joining of others with us. Often we pray alone for our personal needs, and God is pleased to answer. But at times, his means include the leaders of the church, or just the simple prayer of a fellow sinner made righteous in Christ.

7. To Learn and Grow in Our Prayers

Plain and simple, the best way to learn to pray is pray with others who have had their prayers shaped by the Scriptures. Listen for those around you who are acquainted enough with God in prayer as to regularly draw others into communion with him through their praises and petitions. Give careful attention to their approach to God, the kinds of things they thank him for and ask for, and how they keep others in mind in the corporate setting. And beyond what we're conscious of, we're being shaped deep down as we join our hearts with others in prayer.

Some have speculated that the anointing in James 5 is medicinal, and that the instructions are simply to apply the medicine of the day along with prayer. This view seems to overlook the wealth of theology across the Scriptures about the symbolism and significance of anointing—a theology that culminates in Christ himself as the Anointed One (*Christ* means "anointed").

Throughout the Bible, anointing with oil symbolizes consecration to God (Ex. 28:41; Luke 4:18; Acts 4:27; 10:38; 2 Cor. 1:21; Heb. 1:9), with Christ being the greatest manifestation of consecration to God in his perfect human life, sacrificial human death, and victorious human resurrection from the grave. Anointing with oil is an external act of the body that accompanies, and gives expression to, the internal desire and disposition of faith to dedicate someone or something to God in some special way.

Here in James 5, as Douglas Moo writes, "As the elders pray, they are to anoint the sick person in order to symbolize that that person is being set apart for God's special attention and care." Douglas Moo, *The Letter of James, Pillar New Testament Commentary* (Grand Rapids, MI: Eerdmans, 2000), 242. Similar to James 5:14, Mark 6:13 mentions anointing with oil as a means of grace accompanying the apostles' prayer for the sick. The disciples "anointed with oil many who were sick and healed them." It is not automatic in producing healing, but a prayerful expression, and intensifier of prayer to God, asking and waiting for him to heal.

8. To Know Each Other

One of the best ways to get to know fellow believers is by praying together. It is in prayer, in the conscious presence of God, that we're most likely to let the veneer fall. You hear their hearts in prayer like nowhere else. When we pray together, not only do we reveal what most captures our hearts and truly is our treasure, but as we pray together, says Jack Miller, "You can tell if a man or woman is really on speaking terms with God."[5]

9. To Know Jesus More

Saving the best for last, the greatest benefit in praying together is that we know Jesus better when we pray together, in his name, with fellow lovers of him. With our limited vision and perspective, there are parts of Christ we're prone to see with more clarity than others. Our own experiences and personalities emphasize some aspects of his glory and make us blind to others. And so Tim Keller observes, "By praying with friends, you will be able to hear and see facets of Jesus that you have not yet perceived."[6]

And since the great purpose of prayer is not getting things from God but getting God, perhaps this benefit alone will be enough to inspire you to initiate or accept that next opportunity to pray with company.

---

[5] Keller, *Prayer*, 23.
[6] Ibid., 119.

Chapter 10

Sharpen Your Affections
with Fasting

———

Fasting has fallen on hard times—at least, it seems, among our overstuffed bellies in the American church. I speak as one of the well-fed.

Sure, you'll find your exceptions here and there. Some pockets even prize the countercultural enough to steer their vehicles into the ditch of asceticism. But they are vastly outnumbered by the rest of us veering toward the opposite shoulder. The dangers of asceticism are great—surpassed only by those of overindulgence.

Our problem might be how we think of fasting. If the accent is on abstinence, and fasting is some mere duty to perform, then only the most iron-willed among us will get over the social and self-pampering hurdles to actually put this discipline into practice.

But if we are awakened to see fasting for the joy it can bring, as a means of God's grace to strengthen and sharpen godward affections, then we might find ourselves holding a powerful new tool for enriching our enjoyment of Jesus.

What Is Fasting?

Fasting is an exceptional measure, designed to channel and express our desire for God and our holy discontent in a fallen world. It is for those not satisfied with the status quo. For those who want more of God's grace. For those who feel truly desperate for God.

The Scriptures include many forms of fasting: personal and communal, public and private, congregational and national, regular and occasional, partial and absolute. Typically, we think of fasting as voluntarily forgoing food for some limited time, for an express spiritual purpose.

We can fast from good things other than food and drink as well. Martyn Lloyd-Jones said, "Fasting should really be made to include abstinence from anything which is legitimate in and of itself for the sake of some special spiritual purpose."[1] But normal Christian fasting means privately and occasionally choosing to go without food (though not water) for some special period of time (whether a day or three or seven) in view of some specific spiritual purpose.

According to Donald S. Whitney, fasting's spiritual purposes include:

- Strengthening prayer (Ezra 8:23; Joel 2:13; Acts 13:3)
- Seeking God's guidance (Judg. 20:26; Acts 14:23)
- Expressing grief (1 Sam. 31:13; 2 Sam. 1:11–12)
- Seeking deliverance or protection (2 Chron. 20:3–4; Ezra 8:21–23)
- Expressing repentance and returning to God (1 Sam. 7:6; Jonah 3:5–8)
- Humbling oneself before God (1 Kings 21:27–29; Ps. 35:13)

---

[1] D. Martyn Lloyd-Jones, *Studies in the Sermon on the Mount* (Grand Rapids, MI: Eerdmans, 1960), 1:38.

- Expressing concern for the work of God (Neh. 1:3–4; Dan. 9:3)
  - Ministering to the needs of others (Isa. 58:3–7)
  - Overcoming temptation and dedicating yourself to God (Matt. 4:1–11)
  - Expressing love and worship to God (Luke 2:37)[2]

While the potential purposes are many, it is that last one which may be most helpful to focus our thoughts about fasting in this short chapter. It encompasses all the others and gets at the essence of what makes fasting such a mighty means of grace.

Whitney captures it like this: "Fasting can be an expression of finding your greatest pleasure and enjoyment in life from God."[3] And he quotes a helpful phrase from Matthew Henry, who says that fasting serves to "put an edge upon devout affections."

Jesus Assumes We'll Fast

While the New Testament includes no mandate that Christians fast on certain days or with specific frequency, Jesus clearly assumes we will fast. It's a tool too powerful to leave endlessly on the shelf collecting dust. While many biblical texts mention fasting, the two most important come just chapters apart in Matthew's Gospel.

The first is Matthew 6:16–18, which comes in sequence with Jesus's teachings on generosity and prayer:

> And when you fast, do not look gloomy like the hypocrites, for they disfigure their faces that their fasting may be seen by others. Truly, I say to you, they have received their reward. But when you fast, anoint your head and wash your

---

[2] *Spiritual Disciplines for the Christian Life*, rev. ed. (Colorado Springs: NavPress, 2014), 200–17.

[3] Matthew Henry, *Commentary on the Whole Bible* (New York: Funk and Wagnalls, n.d.), 4:1478, quoted in Whitney, *Spiritual Disciplines for the Christian Life*, 214.

face, that your fasting may not be seen by others but by your Father who is in secret. And your Father who sees in secret will reward you.

Fasting is as basic to Christianity as asking from God and giving to others. The key here is that Jesus doesn't say "if you fast," but "when you fast."

The second is Matthew 9:14–15, which may be even more clear. Should Christians today still fast? Jesus's answer is a resounding yes.

Then the disciples of John came to him, saying, "Why do we and the Pharisees fast, but your disciples do not fast?" And Jesus said to them, "Can the wedding guests mourn as long as the bridegroom is with them? The days will come when the bridegroom is taken away from them, and then they will fast." (Matt. 9:14–15)

When Jesus, our bridegroom, was here on earth among his disciples, it was a time for the discipline of feasting.[4] But now that he is "taken away" from his disciples, "they will fast." Not "they might, if they ever get around to it," but "they will." This is confirmed by the pattern of fasting that emerged right away in the early church (Acts 9:9; 13:2; 14:23).

---

[4] Enough could be said about feasting as a spiritual discipline to warrant its own full chapter, but perhaps I can do even better by sending you to Joe Rigney's book-length treatment in *The Things of Earth: Treasuring God by Enjoying His Gifts* (Wheaton, IL: Crossway, 2015). Some readers might suppose that the overstuffed bellies of the American church hardly need any instruction on feasting, since we've grown so accustomed to it, while fasting is the discipline that is grossly underserved. It is true that fasting is largely overlooked and too often forgotten, but true feasting is also in decline through familiarity, overuse, and lack of spiritual purpose. When every day becomes a feast, no day is truly one. We have need to recover the spiritual significance of feasting together in faith—not simply indulging, but explicitly celebrating together, on special occasions, the bounty and kindness of our Creator and Redeemer. For the Christian, our normal daily consumption is to be characterized by enough restraint that feasting is something we can rise to on special occasions, by faith and in good conscience, rather than being the baseline of every day. Daily restraint both keeps our stomachs primed for times of fasting and makes possible a kind of special indulgence on feast days.

Put an Edge on Your Feelings

What makes fasting such a gift is its ability, with the help of the Holy Spirit, to focus our feelings and their expression toward God in prayer. Fasting walks arm in arm with prayer—as John Piper says, fasting is "the hungry handmaiden of prayer," who "both reveals and remedies."

> She reveals the measure of food's mastery over us—or television or computers or whatever we submit to again and again to conceal the weakness of our hunger for God. And she remedies by intensifying the earnestness of our prayer and saying with our whole body what prayer says with the heart: I long to be satisfied in God alone![5]

That burn in your gut, that rolling fire in your belly, aching for you to feed it more food, signals game-time for fasting as a means of grace. Only as we voluntarily embrace the pain of an empty stomach do we see how much we've allowed our belly to be our god (Phil. 3:19).

And in that gnawing discomfort of growing hunger is the engine of fasting, generating the reminder to bend our longings for food godward and inspire intensified longings for Jesus. Fasting, says Piper, is the physical exclamation point at the end of the sentence, "This much, O God, I want you!"[6]

Will You Fast?

More could be said about the rich theology behind Christian fasting, but this habit of grace is simple enough. The question is, will you avail yourself of this potent means of God's grace?

Fasting, like the gospel, isn't for the self-sufficient and those who feel they have it all together. It's for the poor in spirit. It's

---

[5] *When I Don't Desire God: How to Fight for Joy* (Wheaton, IL: Crossway, 2004), 171.
[6] *A Hunger for God*, rev. ed. (Wheaton, IL: Crossway, 2013), 25–26. For a more thorough treatment on fasting, see *A Hunger for God*.

for those who mourn. For the meek. For those who hunger and thirst for righteousness. In other words, fasting is for Christians.

It is a desperate measure, for desperate times, among those who know themselves desperate for God.

———

The Slow Path to Good Fasting

Chances are you are among the massive number of Christians who rarely or never fast. It's not because we haven't read our Bibles or sat under faithful preaching or heard about the power of fasting, or that we don't genuinely want to do it. We just never actually get around to doing it.

Part of it may be that we live in a society in which food is so ubiquitous that we eat not only when we don't need to, but sometimes when we even don't want to. We eat to share a meal with others, to build or grow relationships (which are good reasons), or just from peer pressure.

And of course, there are our own cravings and ache for comfort that keep us from the discomfort of fasting.

When You Fast

Fasting is markedly countercultural in our consumerist society, like abstaining from sex until marriage. If we are to learn the lost art of fasting and enjoy its sweet spiritual fruit, it will not come with our ear to the ground of society but with our Bibles open. Then, our concern will not be whether to fast, but when. As we've seen, Jesus both assumes that his followers will fast, and he promises it will happen. He doesn't say "if," but "when you fast" (Matt. 6:16). And he doesn't say his followers might fast, but "they will" (Matt. 9:15).

We fast in this life because we believe in the life to come. We don't have to get it all here and now, because we have a promise that we will have it all in the age to come. We fast from what we can see and taste, because we have tasted and seen the goodness of the invisible God—and are desperately hungry for more of him.

Radical, Temporary Measure

Fasting is for this world, for stretching our hearts to get fresh air beyond the pain and trouble around us. And it is for the sin and weakness inside us, about which we express our discontent, and long for more of Christ.

When Jesus returns, fasting will be done. It is a temporary measure, for this life and age, to enrich our joy in Jesus and prepare our hearts for the next, and for seeing him face to face. When he returns, he will not call a fast but throw a feast; then all holy abstinence will have served its glorious purpose, and be seen by all for what a gift it was.

But until then, we will fast.

How to Start Fasting

Fasting is hard. It sounds much easier in concept than it proves to be in practice. It can be surprising how on-edge we feel when we miss a meal. Many an idealistic new faster has decided to miss a meal and only found that his belly drove him to make up for it long before the next mealtime came.

Fasting sounds so simple, and yet the world, our flesh, and the Devil conspire to introduce all sorts of complications that keep it from happening. In view of helping you start down the slow path to good fasting, here are six simple pieces of advice. These suggestions might seem pedantic, but my hope is that such basic counsel can serve those who are new at fasting or have never seriously tried it.

1. Start Small

Don't go from no fasting to attempting a weeklong. Start with one meal; maybe fast one meal a week for several weeks. Then try two meals, and work your way up to a daylong fast. Perhaps eventually try a two-day juice fast.

A juice fast means abstaining from all food and beverage, except for juice and water. Allowing yourself juice provides nutrients and sugar for the body to keep you operating while also still feeling the effects from going without solid food. (It is not recommended that you abstain from water during a fast of any length.)

2. Plan What You'll Do Instead of Eating

Fasting isn't merely an act of self-deprivation, but a spiritual discipline for seeking more of God's fullness. Which means we should have a plan for what positive pursuit to undertake in the time it normally takes to eat. We spend a good portion of our day with a fork in hand. One significant part of fasting is the time it creates for prayer and meditation on God's word.

Before diving headlong into a fast, craft a simple plan. Connect it to your purpose for the fast. Each fast should have a specific spiritual purpose. Identify what that is and design a focus to replace your eating time. Without a purpose and plan, it's not Christian fasting; it's just going hungry.

3. Consider How It Will Affect Others

Fasting is no license to be unloving. It would be sad to lack concern and care for others around us because of this expression of heightened focus on God. Love for God and for neighbor go together. Good fasting mingles horizontal concern with the vertical. If anything, others should even feel more loved and cared for when we're fasting.

So as you plan your fast, consider how it will affect others. If you have regular lunches with colleagues or dinners with family or roommates, assess how your abstaining will affect them, and let them know ahead of time, instead of just being a no-show or springing it on them in the moment that you will not be eating.

Also, consider this backdoor inspiration for fasting: If you make a daily or weekly practice of eating with a particular group of friends or family, and those plans are interrupted by someone's travel or vacation or atypical circumstances, consider that as an opportunity to fast, rather than eating alone.

4. TRY DIFFERENT KINDS OF FASTING

The typical form of fasting is personal, private, and partial, but we find a variety of forms in the Bible: personal and communal, private and public, congregational and national, regular and occasional, absolute and partial.

In particular, consider fasting together with your family, small group, or church. Do you share together in some special need for God's wisdom and guidance? Is there an unusual difficulty in the church, or society, for which you need God's intervention? Do you want to keep the second coming of Christ in view? Plead with special earnestness for God's help by linking arms with other believers to fast together.

5. FAST FROM SOMETHING OTHER THAN FOOD

Fasting from food is not necessarily for everyone. Some health conditions keep even the most devout from the traditional course. However, fasting is not limited to abstaining from food, as we saw from Martyn Lloyd-Jones: "Fasting should really be made to include abstinence from anything which is legitimate in and of itself for the sake of some special spiritual purpose."[7]

---

[7] Lloyd-Jones, *Studies in the Sermon on the Mount*, 1:38.

If the better part of wisdom for you, in your health condition, is not to go without food, consider fasting from television, computer, social media, or some other regular enjoyment that would bend your heart toward greater enjoyment of Jesus. Paul even talks about married couples fasting from sex "for a limited time, that you may devote yourselves to prayer" (1 Cor. 7:5).

6. Don't Think of White Elephants

When your empty stomach starts to growl and begins sending your brain every "feed me" signal it can, don't be content to let your mind dwell on the fact that you haven't eaten. If you make it through with an iron will that says no to your stomach but doesn't turn your mind's eye elsewhere, it isn't true fasting.

Christian fasting turns its attention to Jesus or some great cause of his in the world. Christian fasting seeks to take the pains of hunger and transpose them into the key of some eternal anthem, whether it's fighting against some sin, or pleading for someone's salvation, or for the cause of the unborn, or longing for a greater taste of Jesus.

Chapter 11

Journal as a Pathway to Joy

=====

Maybe you've never thought of journaling as a possible means of grace. It's seemed like something for only the most narcissistic of introverts, or cute for adolescent girls, but impractical for adults. *What, me? Journal? I'm much too occupied with today and tomorrow to give any more time to yesterday.* You might be right. Maybe your idea of journaling is too heavy on navel-gazing and too light on real-world value.

But what if there was another vision? What if journaling wasn't simply about recording the past, but preparing for the future? And what if, because of God's grace in our past and his promises for our future, journaling were about deepening your joy in the present?

Perhaps no single new habit would enrich your spiritual life as much as keeping a journal.

No Wrong Way, No Obligation

A good journal really is what you make it. It can be a document on your computer, or just a good old-fashioned notebook. It can be formal or informal, have long entries or short ones, and be a daily stop or just where you pop in on occasion. It can be a place for recording God's providences, peeling at the layers of your own heart, writing out prayers, meditating on Scripture, and dreaming about the future.

The goal is not to leave an impressive catalog of your stunning accomplishments and brilliant insights for future generations to read and admire. Die to that before picking up your pen. The goal is the glory of Christ, not your own, in your ongoing progress in his likeness, for the expanding and enriching of your joy.

Even if many of the Psalms do read like divinely inspired journal entries, nowhere does Scripture command that we keep a journal. Unlike other spiritual disciplines, Jesus left us no model for journaling; he did not keep one.

Journaling is not essential to the Christian life. But it is a powerful opportunity, especially with the technologies we have available today. Many throughout church history and around the world have found journaling to be a regular means of God's grace in their lives.

Why Journal?

With the eyes of faith, the Christian life is a great adventure, and a journal can be greatly beneficial in ripening our joy along the journey. There is always more going on in us and around us than we can appreciate at the time. Journaling is a way of slowing life down for just a few moments, and trying to process at least a sliver of it for the glory of God, our own growth and development, and our enjoyment of the details.

Journaling has the appeal of mingling the motions of our lives with the mind of God. Permeated with prayer and saturated with God's word, it can be a powerful way of hearing God's voice in the Scriptures and making known to him our requests. Think of it as a subdiscipline of Bible intake, and especially of prayer. Let a spirit of prayer pervade, and let God's word inspire, shape, and direct what you ponder and pen.

To Capture the Past

Good journaling is much more than simply capturing the past, but recording past events is one of the most common instincts in it. For the Christian, we acknowledge these as the providences of God. When some important event happens to us, or around us, or some "serendipity" breaks in with divine fingerprints, a journal is a place to capture it and make it available for future reference.

Writing it down provides an opportunity for gratitude and praise to God—not just in the moment, but also one day when we return to what we've recorded. Without capturing some brief record of this good providence or that answer to prayer, we quickly forget the blessing, or the frustration, and miss the chance to see with specificity later on how "'tis grace hath brought me safe thus far," in the words of John Newton's famous hymn. A journal also becomes a place where we can look back not just on what happened, but how we were thinking and feeling about it at the time.

But good journaling isn't just about yesterday; it's also about growing into the future.

To Build a Better Future

It's one thing to think something in a fleeting moment; it's another thing to write it down. As we capture in writing the careful thoughts we're having about God and the Scriptures and ourselves and the world, those impressions are being stamped more deeply on our souls and changing us more in the short term and for the long run.

Journaling is an opportunity to grow into tomorrow. We can

identify where we need to change and set goals and pinpoint priorities and monitor progress. We can evaluate how we're doing in the other habits of grace we want to be practicing.

And the regular discipline of journaling will help you to grow as a communicator and writer, as you practice getting your thoughts into words and onto the page. Your journal is your sandbox, where you can try your hand at daring metaphors and literary flair. It's a safe place to take practice swings before stepping to the plate in public.

To Enrich the Present

Finally, but most significantly, journaling is not just about yesterday and tomorrow, but today, and our joy in the present. Here are three ways, among others, to use journaling to enrich the present.

1. Examine

Socrates overspoke, but was onto something, when he said the unexamined life is not worth living. While limited, there is an important place for introspection and self-examination in the Christian life. For one, it's an opportunity for the Christian to learn "not to think of himself more highly than he ought to think, but to think with sober judgment" (Rom. 12:3). There is a time for examining self (2 Cor. 13:5). Our tendency in journaling is to begin with self-examination, even though we want to move beyond it and see the gospel break in with fresh rays of hope.

An essential part of good journaling is not just self-examination, but getting outside yourself and being caught up in something great—in particular, Someone great. When you're sad or angry or anxious, let your journal begin with your heart's state. Be honest and real, but ask God for the grace to get beyond your circumstances, however bleak, to finding hope in him. This is the frequent pattern in the Psalms: begin harrowed, end hopeful. Journaling is an opportunity to preach the gospel freshly to yourself, beginning where you are, without simply feeding yourself the canned lines of truth you'll default to without pausing to think it over and write it out.

2. Meditate

Think of journaling as the handmaid of that vital Christian discipline we looked at in chapter 3, meditation. This is likely the greatest role journaling can play, alongside prayer, in our practicing the means of grace. Take some juicy bit of gospel from your Bible reading, or a puzzling passage you're stuck on, and let your journal be your laboratory of learning. Pose a hard question, propose a biblical answer, and apply it to your heart and life.

3. Disentangle, Draw Out, and Dream

Finally, as we journal, we're able to disentangle our thoughts, draw out our emotions, and dream about new endeavors. The discipline of writing facilitates careful thinking, catalyzes deep feeling, and inspires intentional action.

Deep joy and satisfaction can come from getting our complicated and confusing thoughts and feelings into words on the page. Our heads and hearts carry around so many unfinished thoughts and emotions we're only able to finish as we write them down. As praise is not just the expression of joy but the consummation of it, so is writing to the soul. Writing doesn't merely capture what's already inside us, but in the very act of writing, we enable our heads and hearts to take the next step, then two, then three. It has a crystallizing effect. Good writing is not just the expression of what we're already experiencing, but the deepening of it.

It is a remarkable thing that God made a world so ready

for written words, and designed human beings so naturally to write them and read them. And he made our minds such that we're able to take thoughts further, and do so in greater detail, than our short-term memory can keep track of in the moment. When we write, we not only disentangle our thoughts, draw out our emotions, and dream about fresh initiatives, but we also develop them.

Journaling, therefore, is not just an exercise in introspection, but a pathway for joy—and a powerful tool in the hands of love.

Five Ways to Flourish in Journaling

Perhaps you're sold on the potential spiritual value of the habit of journaling, but you just don't know how to get going, or keep going.

It can be helpful to hear that there's essentially no wrong way to go about it, and no real rules for it, but that it's something you can really make your own. Be as creative as makes you comfortable. Embrace variety and mix it up as much, or as little, as you prefer. Don't be locked into one way of doing it, and don't be suffocated by someone else's paradigm.

So to help you get going, or keep going, on journal-keeping as a spiritual discipline for the glory of God, the good of others, and the deepening of your own joy, here are five additional pieces of advice for flourishing in this endeavor.

1. Keep It Simple

Journaling is a gift for the long haul. The flash-in-the-pan attempt has limited value. And so an important counsel for journaling is keeping it simple enough that you can keep coming back.

Be modest in your plans for frequency and length of entries. If your expectations are too involved and complex, then you'll be less likely to continue over time. If your only paradigm for journaling requires half an hour or forty-five minutes, then you'll be much less likely to develop the habit than if your expectation is, say, five minutes.

If you're just starting out, or just coming back to the practice, don't try to go from zero to sixty, but take baby steps with regularity. One idea for getting the momentum going is to try writing something short during daily devotions, even just one sentence. I've found that aiming to write just a sentence each day is a helpful way to break long lapses between entries.

2. Don't Catch Up

Even those of us who don't typically think of ourselves as perfectionists can find its magnetic force messing with our journaling radar. It's easy to fall into the mind-set that our journal must contain all the major events, thoughts, and feelings of our lives to really be a journal at all. But that is simply not the case. Journaling should serve your life, not vice versa.

The best of lifelong journals are "incomplete" in that they can't possibly hold everything of significance, or even close—and if their keepers thought they must, then they would have given up long ago. It need not be an exhaustive record of your existence. It must not. It can't.

3. Take God Seriously

Vital to making your journal serve your spiritual vibrancy is saturating it with Scripture and permeating it with prayer. As often as seems natural, make it godward, not only with specific texts from the Bible, but with carefully crafted prayers. Journaling and private prayer can serve as the thermostat for setting our gauges of gravity about Jesus and his providences and our relationship with him.

But don't take yourself too seriously. Don't expect that your records and reflections on life will one day be sought by the general Christian public. It is very likely that no one else will ever read your journal, even your kids after you're dead. Better if they don't. The best of journals are just for yourself and God, without constantly looking over your shoulder to think about what someone else would think if they were reading it. Settle the issue in your own heart now, and write for your own soul's good. Don't alter the course of a lifetime's worth of private journaling just in case someone reads it someday.

Also, not taking yourself too seriously means holding at arm's length your intuitions about and your interpretations of God's providences. Take Scripture with the utmost seriousness, but proceed cautiously when you think you "hear God's voice" or see his direction through various timings and circumstances. Be slow to let one dramatic flurry of journaling inspiration direct a major life decision without carefully testing it over time and in community.

4. Bring the Gospel

Those Christians who flourish in journaling not only pursue prayer, and meditate on Scripture in general, but seek to apply the gospel with specificity to their fears and frustrations, their highs and lows, their joys and sorrows. When you open your journal harrowed, try to follow the path of the psalmists and close with hope. Make 2 Corinthians 4:8–9 come to life as you fill the white space with words. When you feel afflicted, rejoice you're not crushed; when perplexed, drive away despair; when persecuted, remember you're not forsaken; when struck down, know you will not be destroyed.

Your journal is a venue for freshly preaching the gospel to yourself, in your particular circumstances, without parroting the stock lines of truth you'll default to without pausing to meditate. Capture in your own words what you're truly feeling, and then look for God's words that meet your need. Tailor-make the application for today.

5. STAY WITH IT

Even when you make journaling yours and keep it simple and don't bother catching up, there's still the need for persever-ance over the long haul. When the newness wears off and your energy for journaling feels low, remember that it's natural to come against a barrier like this whenever forming a helpful new habit. Ask for God's help to press through the friction, for "the strength that God supplies" (1 Pet. 4:11), for "all his energy that he powerfully works within me" (Col. 1:29).

Often the hardest part is simply sitting down and turning that rusty internal crank to begin letting the words run. But once the door is open, oh how the stream can flow.

Chapter 12

Take a Break from the Chaos

It's surprising how loud silence can be. Especially when you're not used to it. That's my experience each winter, sitting there in the deer stand, the only man-made structure in sight. I am alone in the woods, it is silent—but for the whipping of the frigid Minnesota wind—and my soul is decompressing from months on end in the urban jungle. Body and soul find fresh air there that is hard to come by in the big city.

I want you to join me. Not in the stand (that would ruin it) but in some silent, occasional solitude of your own. You need a break from the chaos, from the noise and the crowds, more than you may think at first. You need the spiritual disciplines of silence and solitude.

Silence and Solitude

We are humans, not machines. We were made for rhythms of silence and noise, community and solitude. It is unhealthy to always have people around, and unhealthy to rarely want them. God made us for cycles and seasons, for routines and cadences.

From the dawn of time, we have needed our respites. Even

the God-man himself was "led by the Spirit into the wilderness" (Matt. 4:1), "went out to a desolate place" (Mark 1:35; Luke 4:42), and "went up on the mountain by himself to pray . . . alone" (Matt. 14:23).

Getting away from time to time has always been a human necessity, but it's all the more pressing in modern life. Especially urban life. By all accounts, things are more crowded, and noisier, than they've ever been.

"One of the costs of technological advancement," says Donald S. Whitney, "is a greater temptation to avoid quietness." And so, many of us "need to realize the addiction we have to noise."[1] Sometimes I catch myself thoughtlessly flipping on the radio every time I get in the car. On occasion I'll turn it off and direct my thoughts godward and pray. In the middle of a busy week, it's remarkable how strange, and wonderful, the silence can be.

And so the excesses and drawbacks of modern life have only increased the value of silence and solitude as spiritual disciplines. Likely we need to get alone and be quiet more than ever before.

Why Get Away?

But merely getting away isn't enough. There is benefit to be had in just letting your spirit decompress and getting out of the concrete jungle, enjoying nature, and letting your soul breathe fresh air. But there's nothing distinctly Christian about that. For those of us who are in Christ, we want to come back better—not only rested, but more ready to love and sacrifice. We want to find new clarity, resolve, and initiative, or return primed to redouble our efforts, by faith, in our callings in the home, among friends, at work, and in the body of Christ.

---

[1] *Spiritual Disciplines for the Christian Life*, rev. ed. (Colorado Springs: NavPress, 2014), 228.

One benefit of silence is simply searching the depths of our own souls, asking what our blind spots have become in the rush of everyday life. In the busyness, is there anything important I'm neglecting or repressing? How am I doing in my various roles? Where do I need to refocus?

Voices in the Silence

We might get alone and be quiet to hear our own internal voice, the murmurs of our soul that are easily drowned out in noise and crowds. But the most important voice to hear in the silence is God's. The point of practicing silence as a spiritual discipline is not so we can hear God's audible voice, but so we can be less distracted and better hear him speak, with even greater clarity, in his word.

Getting away, quiet and alone, is no special grace on its own. But the goal is to create a context for enhancing our hearing from God in his word and responding back to him in prayer. Silence and solitude, then, are not direct means of grace in themselves, but they can grease the skids—like caffeine, sleep, exercise, and singing—for more direct encounters with God in his word and in prayer.

Beware the Dangers

Both silence and solitude have their dangers. They are like fasting, in that we forgo a good gift from God, something for which we were designed, for some limited time, for the sake of some spiritual focus and fruit. Silence and solitude are kinds of fasting, respites from normalcy not meant to take over life.

Silence and solitude are not ideal states, but rhythms of life to steady us for a fruitful return to people and noise. These disciplines are advantageous due to our weaknesses in this present age. It's doubtful we'll need any solitude in the new creation, though there may be the silence of worship (Rev. 8:1). The book of Revelation makes heaven seem loud and crowded, in all the best ways.

Solitude is a kind of companion to fellowship, a fasting from other people, to make our return to them all the better. And silence is a fasting from noise and talk, to improve our listening and speaking. But God doesn't mean for us to fast long from food, fellowship, noise, and talk. And there's nothing in Scripture that would lead us to think he would have us ever fast from his word and prayer. In fact, it is increased engagement with God's word and prayer that is at the heart of good silence and solitude.

Make Room for Daily Respites

Most talk about silence and solitude as spiritual disciplines seems to imply some kind of special retreat from normal life, but small, daily "retreats" can be vital as well. Such a brief season, alone and quiet, for hearing God's voice in his word and responding to him in prayer, may be most fruitful in the morning when we are rested and alert, and the chaos of the day isn't snowballing around us yet.

Some Christians have called it a "quiet time," highlighting the silence; others, "time alone with God," emphasizing the solitude. Call it what you may, these short daily stretches of engaging directly with God in the Scriptures and prayer are possible amid the chaos of modern life, and invaluable in guarding our heads and hearts in a noisy, crowded world.

Schedule a Special Retreat

It can be fruitful to set aside special retreats as well. In my current season of life as a young parent, about all that's realistic for me is a long weekend in the deer stand once a year. Ideally, such a get-away might be something you do twice a year, or even once a quarter. It can be inside or out, totally alone (miles from any other human) or at the same facility or center as others, practicing "solitude together" at your own stations. Details will vary, but I commend the general habit for your soul—and doubt it will happen for you without some proactivity and initiative to plan ahead.

When you do get such a thing on the calendar and find a place for it, here are some ideas for how to move through such a special season of silence and solitude.

- Pray for God's blessing, that he will bring to light what in life needs your fresh attention, and that his Spirit will prompt your subconscious to "speak" honestly to your soul. Don't assume the voices in your head are God's; assume they are yours. To hear God, take up the Scriptures, and to the degree that your own thoughts for yourself align with what God has revealed in his word, then take them as a gift from God and take them to heart.
- Read and meditate on the Bible, whether it's what's assigned that day in some regular reading plan you're working through in your daily respites or some special section you've selected for your time away. Trust God to meet you in his word and lead your time with Scripture—not just with internal promptings, but in what his providence has put before you objectively in the Bible.
- Perhaps spend a few minutes just listening to the silence, and let your soul begin to "thaw," especially if you keep a busy schedule in a crowded town.
- Have a computer (consider turning the Wi-Fi off!) or good old-fashioned pen and paper. After thawing out, get the voices in your head down on paper (the silence and solitude of a special retreat provide a great context for the spiritual discipline of journaling we discussed in chap. 11).

- Resist the urge to get detailed right away about specific to-dos back home; try to reflect on life and your callings in the big picture, at least to begin with. But as you wrap up your time away, get more specific, and bring back with you into normal life some takeaways that will help you sense, even immediately, the value of your retreat.
- During your time away, include an extended season of prayer, guided by the Scriptures, perhaps the Lord's Prayer, and continue recording thoughts as you direct your heart godward in praise, confession, petition, and supplication.
- Consider setting a calendar reminder for a few days or a week after you return home to reflect back on your time away and read any notes you took or journaling you got on paper.

You may not know how badly you needed silence and solitude until you get to know them.

Part 3

BELONG TO HIS BODY

Fellowship

Chapter 13

Learn to Fly in the Fellowship

═════

It's a shame the word "fellowship" has fallen on hard times in some circles, and is dying the death of domestication and triviality. It is an electric reality in the New Testament, an indispensable ingredient in the Christian faith, and one of God's chief means of grace in our lives.

The *koinonia*—Greek for commonality, partnership, fellowship—that the first Christians shared wasn't anchored in a common love for pizza, pop, and a nice clean evening of fun among the fellow churchified. Its essence was in their common Christ, and their common life-or-death mission together in his summons to take the faith worldwide in the face of impending persecution.

Rightly did Tolkien call his nine "the Fellowship of the Ring." This is no chummy hobnob with apps and drinks and a game on the tube. It is an all-in, life-or-death collective venture in the face of great evil and overwhelming opposition. True fellowship is less like friends gathered to watch the Super Bowl and more like players on the field in blood, sweat, and tears, huddled in the backfield only in preparation for the next down.

True fellowship, in this age, is more the invading troops side by side on the beach at Normandy than it is the gleeful revelers in the street on V-E Day.

Partnership for the Gospel

Not only did the first Christians devote themselves to the word (the apostles' teaching) and to prayer, but also to "fellowship" (Acts 1:14; 2:42). Foremost, their fellowship was in Jesus (1 Cor. 1:9) and in his Spirit (2 Cor. 13:14). In Christ, they had become fellow heirs of the divine inheritance (Rom. 8:17; Eph. 3:6), soon they shared "all things in common" (Acts 2:44; 4:32), and even Jew and Gentile now were fellow citizens (Eph. 2:19). From top to bottom, the gospel creates community like no other.

But this fellowship is no isolated commune or static, mutual-admiration society. It is a "partnership in the gospel" (Phil. 1:5), among those giving their everything to "advance the gospel" (1:12), knit together for "progress and joy in the faith" (1:25). It is the fellowship in which, as Paul says to Christians, "you are all partakers with me of grace . . . in the defense and confirmation of the gospel" (1:7).

In such a partnership as this, we need not worry too much that we will forget the lost and sequester the gospel. Real fellowship will do precisely the opposite. It must. The same Jesus who joins us commissions us. The medium of our relationship is the message of salvation. When the fellowship is true, the depth of love for each other is not a symptom of in-growth, but the final apologetic: "By this all people will know that you are my disciples, if you have love for one another" (John 13:35).

The Twin Texts of Fellowship

But true fellowship not only labors to win the lost, but serves to keep fellow saints saved. The relational iceberg, lying just beneath the surface of the Scriptures, is especially close to sea level in Hebrews. Here rise the twin texts of Christian fellowship, stationed as guardians of the heart of the epistle, lest we try to access grace as isolated individuals. Perhaps the better known is Hebrews 10:24–25:

> Let us consider how to stir up one another to love and good works, not neglecting to meet together, as is the habit of some, but encouraging one another, and all the more as you see the Day drawing near.

The remarkable thing here is not the summons to keep meeting together, but the instruction that when you do, look past your own nose to the needs of others. There's no "how" here in the original language. A literal translation is: "*Consider each other* for love and good deeds." Know each other. Get close. Stay close. Go deep. And *consider* particular persons, and interact with them, such that you exhort and inspire them to love and good deeds specifically fitting to their mix.[1]

Here we taste how potent, and personal, is fellowship as a means of grace. As partners under God's word and in prayer, a brother who knows me as me, and not generic humanity, speaks the truth in love (Eph. 4:15) into my life, and gives me a word "such as is good for building up, as fits the occasion, that it may give grace to those who hear" (Eph. 4:29). This is an inestimable grace.

Be the Means for Your Brother

The twin, then, is Hebrews 3:12–13:

> Take care, brothers, lest there be in any of you an evil, unbelieving heart, leading you to fall away from the living God.

---

[1] For more on giving and receiving exhortation and reproof, see chapter 18.

> But exhort one another every day . . . that none of you may
> be hardened by the deceitfulness of sin.

Here the charge lands not on the drifting saint to get himself back on the path, but on the others in the community—to have enough proximity to him, awareness of him, and regularity with him to spot the drift and war with him, for him, against the sin. This means of grace, then, in such a circumstance, has a unique function in the Christian life. It is not laid on the spiritually weak to muster their will and do the discipline, but it is for the body to take up discipline on behalf of the wanderer, to mediate grace to the struggler, to preempt apostasy by putting words of truth and grace into his open ear hole and praying for the Spirit to make them live.

The Glorious Backstop of Grace

Fellowship may be the often forgotten middle child of the spiritual disciplines, but she may save your life in the dark night of your soul. As you pass through the valley of the shadow of death, and the Shepherd comforts you with his staff, you will discover that he has fashioned his people to act as his rod of rescue. When the desire to avail yourself of hearing his voice (in the word) has dried up, and when your spiritual energy is gone to speak into his ear (in prayer), God sends his body to bring you back. It is typically not the wanderer's own efforts that prompt his return to the fold, but his brothers' (James 5:19–20), being to him a priceless means of God's grace—the invaluable backstop.

It is not only God's word and prayer that are the means of his ongoing grace, but true fellowship among those who have in common the one who is Grace incarnate (Titus 2:11). The grace of God cannot be quarantined to individuals. The healthy Christian, introverted or not, of whatever temperament, in whatever season, seeks not to minimize relationships with his fellows in Christ but maximize them.

God has given us each other in the church, not just for company and cobelligerency, not just to chase away loneliness and lethargy, but to be to each other an indispensable means of his divine favor. We are for each other an essential element of the good work God has begun in us and promises to bring to completion (Phil. 1:6).

Such is the true fellowship.

———

Making Fellowship Official

One thing to make explicit here at the end of this first chapter on fellowship, and the beginning of part 3 on the means of grace in the church, is that the deepest, most durable form of fellowship is covenantal—in other words, it is between parties that have made formal commitments to each other. This is not only true in the partnership of marriage, but also in the local church. When we make vows and promises to each other in covenanting together in a local church as "members" or "partners" (or whatever term a church uses), we don't inhibit the true life of the church, but give the truest conditions for its growth and flourishing.

When our fellowship is not simply a network of loose Christian relationships, but anchored in a particular "covenant community" as committed members together in a local outpost of Christ's kingdom, we come closest to experiencing what those first Christians did, when people didn't just drift in and out of the community, but were either in or out—and those who were in were pledged to be the church for each other through thick and thin. Covenant community is like Christian marriage in that it is within the framework of stated commitments and promised allegiances that life in relationship is guarded, nourished, and encouraged most to thrive.[2]

———

Six Lessons in Good Listening

Let's close this chapter by considering the importance of listening, and how this underrated act, which is essential for fellowship, serves as a means of grace both to ourselves and to others in the life of the church. Listening is one of the easiest things you'll ever do, and one of the hardest. In a sense, listening is easy—or *hearing* is easy. It doesn't demand the initiative and energy required in speaking. That's why "faith comes from hearing, and hearing through the word of Christ" (Rom. 10:17). The point is that hearing is easy, and faith is not an expression of our activity, but our receiving the activity of another. It is "hearing with faith" (Gal. 3:2, 5) that accents the achievements of Christ and thus is the channel of grace that starts and sustains the Christian life.

But despite this ease—or perhaps precisely because of it—we often fight against it. In our sin, we'd rather trust in ourselves than another, amass our own righteousness than receive another's, speak our own mind rather than listen to someone else. True, sustained, active listening is a great act of faith, and a great means of grace, both for ourselves and for others in the fellowship.

The charter text for Christian listening might be James 1:19: "Let every person be quick to hear, slow to speak, slow to anger." It's simple enough in principle, and nearly impossible to live. Too often we are slow to hear, quick to speak, and

---

[2] For more on the nature and importance of church membership, see my short article, "Why Join a Church," http://www.desiringGod.org/articles/why-join-a-church.

quick to anger. So learning to listen well won't happen overnight. It requires discipline, effort, and intentionality. You get better with time, people say. Becoming a better listener hangs not on one big resolve to do better in a single conversation, but on developing a pattern of little resolves—cultivating the habit—to focus in on particular people in specific moments.

Freshly persuaded this is a needed area of growth in my life—and possibly yours as well—here are six lessons in good listening. (We take our cues from what may be the most important three paragraphs on listening outside the Bible, the section on "the ministry of listening" in Dietrich Bonhoeffer's *Life Together*, as well as Janet Dunn's classic *Discipleship Journal* article, "How to Become a Good Listener."[3])

1. Good Listening Requires Patience

Here Bonhoeffer gives us something to avoid: "a kind of listening with half an ear that presumes already to know what the other person has to say." This, he says, "is an impatient, inattentive listening, that . . . is only waiting for a chance to speak." We might think we know where the speaker is going, and so already begin formulating our response. Or we were in the middle of something when someone started talking to us, or have another commitment approaching, and we wish they were done already.

Or maybe we're half-eared because our attention is divided by our external surroundings or our internal focus returning to self. As Dunn laments, "Unfortunately, many of us are too preoccupied with ourselves when we listen. Instead of concentrating on what is being said, we are busy either deciding what to say in response or mentally rejecting the other person's point of view."

---

[3] Bonhoeffer, *Life Together: The Classic Exploration of Faith in Community* (New York: HarperOne, 2009), 97–99. Dunn's article is available at desiringGod.org, http://www.desiringgod.org/articles/how-to-become-a-good-listener.

Positively, then, good listening requires concentration and means we're in with both ears, and that we hear the other person out till he's done speaking. Rarely will the speaker begin with what's most important, and deepest. We need to hear the whole train of thought, all the way to the caboose, before starting across the tracks.

Good listening silences the smartphone and doesn't stop the story, but is attentive and patient. It is externally relaxed and internally active. It takes energy to block out the distractions that keep bombarding us, and the peripheral things that keep streaming into our consciousness, and the many good excuses we might have for interrupting. When we are people quick to speak, it takes Spirit-powered patience to not only be quick to hear, but to keep on hearing.

2. Good Listening Is an Act of Love

Half-eared listening, says Bonhoeffer, "despises the brother and is only waiting for a chance to speak and thus get rid of the other person." Poor listening rejects; good listening embraces. Poor listening diminishes others, while good listening invites them to exist, and to matter. Bonhoeffer writes, "Just as love to God begins with listening to his Word, so the beginning of love for the brethren is learning to listen to them."

Good listening goes hand in hand with the mind-set of Christ (Phil. 2:5). It flows from a humble heart that counts others more significant than ourselves (Phil. 2:3). It looks not only to its own interests, but also the interests of others (Phil. 2:4). It is patient and kind (1 Cor. 13:4).

3. Good Listening Asks Perceptive Questions

This counsel is writ large in Proverbs. It is the fool who "takes no pleasure in understanding, but only in exercising his opinions" (18:2), and thus "gives an answer before he hears" (18:13). "The purpose in a man's heart is like deep water," says Proverbs 20:5, "but a man of understanding will draw it out."

Good listening asks perceptive, open-ended questions that don't just tee up yes-no answers but gently peel the onion and probe beneath the surface. It watches carefully for nonverbal communication, but doesn't interrogate and pry into details the speaker doesn't want to share. It meekly draws them out and helps point the speaker to fresh perspectives through careful, but genuine, leading questions.

4. Good Listening Is Ministry

According to Bonhoeffer, there are many times when "listening can be a greater service than speaking." God wants more of the Christian than just our good listening, but not less. There will be days when the most important ministry we do is square our shoulders to some hurting person, uncross our arms, lean forward, make eye contact, and hear his pain all the way to the bottom. Says Dunn,

> Good listening often defuses the emotions that are a part of the problem being discussed. Sometimes releasing these emotions is all that is needed to solve the problem. The speaker may neither want nor expect us to say anything in response.

One of Dunn's counsels for cultivating good listening is: "Put more emphasis on affirmation than on answers. . . . Many times God simply wants to use me as a channel of his affirming love as I listen with compassion and understanding." Echoes Bonhoeffer, "Often a person can be helped merely by having someone who will listen to him seriously." At times what our neighbor needs most is for someone else to know, because we care enough to listen.

5. GOOD LISTENING PREPARES US TO SPEAK WELL

Sometimes good listening only listens, and ministers best by keeping quiet (for the moment), but typically good listening readies us to minister words of grace to precisely the place where the other is in need. As Bonhoeffer writes, "We should listen with the ears of God that we may speak the Word of God."

While the fool "gives an answer before he hears" (Prov. 18:13), the wise person tries to resist defensiveness, and to listen from a nonjudgmental stance, training himself not to formulate opinions or responses until the full account is on the table and the whole story has been heard.

6. GOOD LISTENING REFLECTS OUR RELATIONSHIP WITH GOD

Our inability to listen well to others may be symptomatic of a chatty spirit that is drowning out the voice of God. Bonhoeffer warns,

> He who can no longer listen to his brother will soon be no longer listening to God either; he will be doing nothing but prattle in the presence of God too. This is the beginning of the death of the spiritual life. . . . Anyone who thinks that his time is too valuable to spend keeping quiet will eventually have no time for God and his brother, but only for himself and for his own follies.

Good listening is a great means of grace in the dynamic of true Christian fellowship. Not only is it a channel through which God continues to pour his grace into our lives, but it's also his way of using us as his means of grace in the lives of others. Cultivating habits of good listening may be one of the hardest things we learn to do, but we will find it worth every ounce of grace-empowered effort.

Chapter 14

Kindle the Fire in Corporate Worship

———

We were made for more than private devotions. As nice as it can be to tuck ourselves away in some nook and cranny, all by our lonesome, and read the Scriptures we want to read, pray the prayers we prefer, play the songs we like, memorize the verses we pick, and fast from food when it's convenient—as important as it is to pursue a regular rhythm of "private worship" in these personal disciplines—this is not the pinnacle of our Christian lives.

We were made to worship Jesus *together*. Among the multitude. With the great horde. Swallowed up in the magnificent mass of the redeemed. God didn't fashion us to enjoy him finally as solitary individuals, but as happy members of a countlessly large family.

When the fog of everyday life clears and we catch a glimpse of heaven's bliss, we don't find ourselves sequestered at a study desk or hidden alone in a prayer closet in paradise, or even standing alone before the great Grand Canyon or mountain peak of God's majesty, but joyfully part of the worshiping throng of Christ's people from every tongue and tribe and nation.

We were made for *corporate* worship.

Cheerfully Part of the Crowd

Heaven will be more spectacular than we can dream—and the new earth, even better than heaven—but it might be surprising to hear that perhaps the best foretaste we can get on this side is with the gathered church, worshiping Jesus together. This doesn't mean that eternity will amount to an unending church service, but that we will be wonderfully immersed in a joy-multiplying multitude of fellow worshipers.

And in heaven's adoration, we join not only "many angels, numbering myriads of myriads and thousands of thousands" (Rev. 5:11; cf. Heb. 12:22), worshiping Jesus with "innumerable angels" (Heb. 12:22), but also the innumerable communion of the ransomed:

> A great multitude that no one could number, from every nation, from all tribes and peoples and languages, standing before the throne and before the Lamb . . . and crying out with a loud voice, "Salvation belongs to our God who sits on the throne, and to the Lamb!" (Rev. 7:9–10)

While the corporate worship of Jesus by the church *universal* is an essential element in our great destiny, it is the corporate worship of Jesus by the church *local* that is a vital means of God's grace in getting us there.

The Most Important Means of Grace

Corporate worship is the single most important means of grace and our greatest weapon in the fight for joy, because like no other means, corporate worship combines all three principles of God's ongoing grace: his word, prayer, and fellowship. It is corporate worship, with its preaching and sacraments and collective praises, confessions, petitions, and thanksgivings, which most acutely brings together the gifts of God's voice, his ear, and his body.

And so, according to Donald S. Whitney, "There's an element of worship and Christianity that cannot be experienced in private worship or by watching worship. There are some graces and blessings that God gives only in 'meeting together' with other believers."[1]

Perhaps your own experience of corporate worship as a means of grace has, at times, echoed that of Martin Luther: "At home, in my own house, there is no warmth or vigor in me, but in the church when the multitude is gathered together, a fire is kindled in my heart and it breaks its way through."[2]

Worship Is No Means

But talking about worship as a means of grace is tricky, because, as John Piper cautions us, true worship is not a means to anything.

> Worship is an end in itself. We do not eat the feast of worship as a means to anything else. Happiness in God [which is the heart of worship] is the end of all our seeking. Nothing beyond it can be sought as a higher goal. . . . True worship cannot be performed as a means to some other experience.[3]

---

[1] *Spiritual Disciplines for the Christian Life*, rev. ed. (Colorado Springs: NavPress, 2014), 111.
[2] Quoted in *Worship by the Book*, ed. D. A. Carson (Grand Rapids, MI: Zondervan, 2002), 159–60.
[3] *Desiring God: Meditations of a Christian Hedonist*, rev. ed. (Colorado Springs: Multnomah, 2011), 90.

What, then, do we mean when we say that corporate worship is an essential *means of God's grace*? Can it really be such?

The Secret of Joy: Self-Forgetfulness

One important distinction to make is between the essence of worship as joy in God and the context of corporate worship as the gathered assembly. While praising Jesus together is its greatest specific expression, worship in general is bigger than just the gathered church—it is not just for Sunday mornings, but for everyday life (Rom. 12:1). And related to this is the distinction between how we think about corporate worship (and the various motivations for it and benefits from it) and how we experience it in the moment.

There is more to be said (and will be below) about the "graces and blessings that God gives only in 'meeting together' with other believers," which can inspire our faithful engagement and help us appreciate the irreplaceable role corporate worship plays in our Christian health and growth. But first, the question is, where should we turn our hearts and minds collectively *in the moment* of corporate worship to experience this grace from God?

The answer is that we should not be self-consciously preoccupied with how we're being strengthened or what grace we're receiving. Rather, our focus together is the crucified and risen Christ and the incomparable excellencies of his person and work (which illumines all the means of grace and various spiritual disciplines, not only corporate worship—and is why the subtitle of this book begins with "enjoying Jesus"). Corporate worship is a means of grace not when we're caught up with what we're doing, but when we experience the secret of worship—the joy of self-forgetfulness—as we become preoccupied together with Jesus and his manifold perfections.

See, then, the pregnant application to corporate worship in this summary by Piper:

All genuine emotion is an end in itself. It is not consciously caused as a means to something else. This does not mean we cannot or should not seek to have certain feelings. We should and we can. We can put ourselves in situations [like corporate worship] where the feeling may more readily be kindled. . . . But *in the moment of authentic emotion, the calculation vanishes*. We are transported (perhaps only for seconds) above the reasoning work of the mind, and we experience feeling without reference to logical or practical implications.[4]

In this way, corporate worship, which in one sense is no means to anything else, is a powerful—even the most powerful—means of God's grace for the Christian life.

So come to corporate worship for the many blessings, and then let the calculations vanish as you lose yourself in the Blessed. Get yourself there on a slow day with a reminder about how good it will be for you if you do, and as the gathering begins, go hard after the goodness of God and seek to forget yourself as you focus on his Son.

———

Five Benefits of Corporate Worship

I don't want to leave you in the dark about what some of those "graces and blessings" of corporate worship might be. Surely many more could be given, but here are five such blessings that we experience uniquely in the context of corporate worship.

1. Awakening

Often we come into corporate worship feeling a sense of spiritual fog. During the rough-and-tumble of the week, the hard

---

[4] Ibid., 92. Emphasis added.

knocks of real life in the fallen world can disorient us to ultimate reality and what's truly important. We need to clear our heads, recalibrate our spirits, and jump-start our slow hearts. We mentioned above how Martin Luther found corporate worship powerful in awakening his spiritual fire: "At home, in my own house, there is no warmth or vigor in me, but in the church when the multitude is gathered together, a fire is kindled in my heart and it breaks its way through."

Better than Luther, though, is the experience of the inspired psalmist. In Psalm 73, he begins by despairing over the prosperity of his wicked peers (vv. 2–15). But the fog clears as he comes consciously into the presence of God: "When I thought how to understand this, it seemed to me a wearisome task, until I went into the sanctuary of God; then I discerned their end" (Ps. 73:16–17).

He was embattled. The spiritual haze was thick. But the breakthrough came in the context of worship, which then led to this climactic expression of praise: "Whom have I in heaven but you? And there is nothing on earth that I desire besides you. My flesh and my heart may fail, but God is the strength of my heart and my portion forever" (Ps. 73:25–26).

I've found this to be true for me more times than I can count. Instead of staying away from corporate worship when we sense ourselves to be spiritually lethargic, precisely what we need more than ever is the awakening of worship. When our hearts feel it least is when we need most to remind our souls, "For me it is good to be near God" (Ps. 73:28).

2. Assurance

A second benefit is the community dynamic—which means not only meeting our good desires for belonging and shared mission (fellowship), but also providing a catalyst for our assurance.

While we may admire figures like Athanasius and Luther who seemingly stood alone *contra mundum* ("against the world"), we must remember God has said it is not good for us to be alone (Gen. 2:18). Such heroes were the product of dire days, and inevitably their stories have been thinned in the collective memory of distant history. Neither Athanasius nor Luther truly stood alone, but were part of faithful communities that fostered and strengthened their otherwise unpopular beliefs.

And so it is with us. We were not made to stand solo with no fellows. Even in times as troubling as Elijah's, God gave him seven thousand who hadn't abandoned the truth (1 Kings 19:18). God made us for community—and named her "the church"— and being part of this great local and global community plays an important role in assuring us not only that we are not deceiving ourselves in pretending our profession is credible, but also that we truly know whom we have believed (2 Tim. 1:12).

And worship in the local church points us to the worship of the universal church, and that Jesus has a people from many nations, and one day will include every nation (Rev. 7:9).

3. Advance

Corporate worship also plays an indispensible part in our sanctification—our progressive growth in being conformed to the image of Jesus (Rom. 8:29). Corporate worship is for our general "upbuilding and encouragement and consolation" (1 Cor. 14:3), but also in beholding Jesus together, "we all . . . are being transformed into the same image from one degree of glory to another" (2 Cor. 3:18).

Christian growth is not just something that we take away as sermon application and then work into our lives that week. As Tim Keller says, sanctification can happen "on the spot" as we sit under gospel preaching and engage in corporate worship. There are times—may God make them many—when the Holy Spirit takes the Scripture read, the prayer spoken, the chorus sung, or the truth preached and presses it right to the point of our need. Corporate worship does not merely inform our Christian walk, but heals us or transforms us in that moment.

When we join in corporate worship, God loves not only to change our minds, but to irrevocably change our hearts right then and there.

4. Accepting Another's Leading

One important distinction between public worship and the "private worship" of personal Bible intake and prayer is the place of our initiative. Corporate worship reminds us that our faith is fundamentally receptive, not of our own initiative. In private devotions, we lead ourselves in some sense. In corporate worship, we're made to receive the leading of others.

In private worship, we're in the driver's seat, in some sense. We decide what passage to read, when to pray, what to pray, how long to linger in Bible reading and meditation, what songs to listen to or sing, what gospel truths to preach to ourselves, and what applications to consider. But in corporate worship, we respond. We follow. Others preach and pray and select the songs and choose how long to linger in each element. We're positioned to receive.

It is a wonderful thing in our personal devotions to make such choices, but it is also good for us to practice engaging with God when someone other than ourselves is making the calls. Corporate worship demands that we discipline ourselves to respond, and not only pursue God on our own terms. It is an opportunity to embrace being led, and not always taking the lead.

5. Accentuated Joy

Last, but not least, is the heightened experience of worship in the corporate context. Our own awe is accentuated, our own adoration increased, our own joy doubled when we worship Jesus *together*.

As the Swedish proverb says, *a shared joy is a double joy*. In corporate worship, the "graces and benefits" we uniquely enjoy are not only awakening, assurance, advance, and accepting others' leadership, but also the accentuated joy of deeper and richer and greater adoration and awe, since our delight in Jesus expands as we magnify him together with others.

The secret of joy in corporate worship is not only self-forgetfulness—or to put it positively, preoccupation with Jesus and his glory—but also the happy awareness that we are not alone in having our souls satisfied in him.

Chapter 15

Listen for Grace in the Pulpit

=====

Few practices will energize and affect your Christian life as much as sitting attentively under faithful preaching.

While corporate worship as a whole may be the single most important means of God's grace, as we said in chapter 14, hearing the fresh preaching of the gospel from the Scriptures is the climactic grace of that gathering. It is that moment among the assembled church when God speaks in monologue most clearly and completely. The other elements of the gathering follow the rhythm of receiving from him and responding back to him, but in preaching we move into the posture of simply receiving, whether it's a full half hour or just a tight twenty minutes.

The weekly priority of preaching in worship points to the importance of our not just interacting with God as friends and sharing at his Table as family, but also submitting to his word in the message of his herald, the preacher. Time abounds elsewhere to ask questions and respond, and seasons multiply to converse and dialogue. But preaching is that one half hour each week when the assembly of the redeemed closes her collective mouth, opens her ears and heart, and hears the uninterrupted voice of her husband, through his appointed mouthpiece, fallible though the messenger be.

The Discipline of Listening

But even when we have another 112 or so waking hours each week to do and discuss and dialogue and debate, it's still easy to be restless for these thirty minutes. We love the idea of equality, and we're accustomed to listening on our own terms. We prize conversations; we adore dialogue. And dialogue is essential in disciplemaking. The Great Commission goes forward through great conversations. There are times to interact with our Groom, and times for *us* to speak at length in prayer and in song. But there are also times for us to sit and listen quietly and intently.

When we put ourselves under the preaching of God's word, it is one of the precious few moments in life today when we close our mouths and resist the temptation to respond right away, and focus our energy and attention to hearing with faith.

The Pulpit's Picture of God's Love

The act of preaching itself is a picture of the gospel. As the preacher stands behind the Book, doing his level best to reveal Jesus afresh to his people, our Lord is put on display, not for give-and-take and the mingling of our efforts together in some mutual enterprise. Rather, we sit in the seat of weakness and desperation. What we need is not some boost from a trusted fellow to get us over the wall, but the rescue of the Savior for the utterly helpless.

This is why when God's own Son took human flesh and blood and dwelt among us, fully one of us, he came preaching. The greatness of God and the gravity of our sin come together to give preaching its essential place. Endless dialogue, without a pause for preaching, betrays both the direness of our situation and the depth of God's mercy.

And so Jesus was sent not only to die as the remedy, but to preach (Luke 4:43). Jesus himself is the person the Scriptures most often refer to as *preaching*. And he sent out his disciples to preach (Mark 3:14). Jesus was the consummate preacher, but after his ascension, the preaching doesn't disappear. When we turn to Acts, it's as alive and well as ever. The preaching of the Groom extends into the life of the church.

A Preoccupation with Jesus

Jesus didn't just display the importance of preaching in his life, but he is the focal point of all faithful preaching in the church. Just as our focus together in the whole of corporate worship is the crucified and risen Christ and the incomparable excellencies of his person and work, so also is the focus of our preaching.

The best of preaching serves the worshiper in the joy of self-forgetfulness, and preacher-forgetfulness. Preaching that goes on and on about the preacher himself, or is always angling at how the hearer should apply this or that to daily life, does so at the expense of tapping into the very power of preaching, namely, a preoccupation with Jesus. True Christian preaching swallows up the listener again and again not with self or the speaker, but with Jesus and his manifold perfections.

There is a place for the preacher's self-disclosure and for making the plain connections to practical application, but not at the expense of Jesus and his gospel as the sermon's crescendo and culmination. The waters of good preaching are always running downhill to the stream of Christ, who he is, and how he has loved us.

Present with His Church

But preaching is not just about Jesus; it is his way of being personally present with his church. Good preaching brings the church into an encounter with her Groom by the Holy Spirit. As Jason Meyer writes, "The ministry of the word in Scripture is stewarding and heralding God's word in such a way that people *encounter God* through his word."[1] In faithful Christian preaching, we not only hear about Jesus, but we meet him.

Preaching not only communicates truths *about* God, but serves the function of "conveying the very presence *of* God." It is to be valued not merely for its exegetical insights, but "for its role as a means through which God truly speaks and in which Christ is really present."[2] While preaching has not technically been called an "ordinance" or "sacrament" (like baptism and the Lord's Supper; more on those in the next two chapters), its power is *sacramental*. It is a God-appointed means of communicating his grace to the church through the channel of our faith, with the chief benefit being an encounter with Jesus himself.

Experience the Joy

The point of preaching, as John Calvin captures it, is "to offer and set forth Christ to us, and in him the treasures of heavenly grace."[3] In the preaching of God's word, says Marcus Peter Johnson, "God himself speaks and is present to us through his Son in the power of the Spirit to bless and nourish us."[4]

The great goal of preaching, as well as the sacraments and our various other habits of grace, as we have seen, is *knowing*

---

[1] *Preaching: A Biblical Theology* (Wheaton, IL: Crossway, 2013), 21.
[2] Marcus Peter Johnson, *One with Christ: An Evangelical Theology of Salvation* (Wheaton, IL: Crossway, 2013), 220.
[3] John Calvin, *Institutes of the Christian Religion*, ed. John T. McNeill, trans. Ford Lewis Battles, 2 vols., The Library of Christian Classics 20–21 (Philadelphia: Westminster, 1960), 4.14.17, quoted in Johnson, *One with Christ*, 219.
[4] Johnson, *One with Christ*, 221.

and enjoying Jesus. The greatest incentive for attentive listening as we gather for corporate worship and sit under the preaching of God's word is *that we may know him* (Phil. 3:10).

Here we taste eternal life for thirty minutes a week in the highest aim of Christian preaching: that we know the only true God, and Jesus Christ whom he has sent (John 17:3).

———

Five Graces in Faithful Preaching

To whet your appetite with specificity for next Sunday, here are five specific graces, among many more, some already plain in this chapter and some fresh, of sitting with faith under the faithful preaching of God's word.

1. To Forget Ourselves

One of the great blessings of good preaching is that it helps us in the life-giving act of self-forgetfulness. Faithful preaching exposes our sin and challenges us to change, but it does so in the stanzas, while the chorus calls us away from self to the Savior. It is a glorious thing for our souls to be freed from our regular preoccupation with self, even if for only a few moments at the sermon's climax, as we're captivated by Christ.

2. To Fill Our Faith

Faithful preaching refills our faith. Personal renewal and steady-state strengthening come not from giving ourselves a pep talk but from regularly receiving the preaching of the gospel. We simply don't have the resources in and of ourselves. We need an external word. "Faith comes from hearing, and hearing through the word of Christ" (Rom. 10:17).

Our souls are strengthened by the preached gospel, as Paul prays in his doxology at the end of Romans: "Now to him who is able to strengthen you according to my gospel and the preaching of Jesus Christ . . ." (16:25). The message of the cross is folly to the perishing, but it is the wisdom of God to those who believe—and power for the Christian life (1 Cor. 1:18–24). And according to 1 Corinthians 15:1–2, the preached gospel is not only what we have received in the past to become Christians, but it is that grace in which we presently stand, and that by which we will be finally saved, if we continue to receive and hold onto this gospel. The ongoing preaching of the gospel is vital to the ongoing life of faith.

3. To Grow in Grace

When we sit attentively under the faithful preaching of the gospel, not only do we forget ourselves and refill our faith, but we are genuinely changed. The gospel we preach is the fragrance from life to life, or death to death (2 Cor. 2:15–16). We grow or shrivel. Our hearts warm or cool. We soften or become callous. There is no neutrality when the preaching sounds.

As we noted in the previous chapter, Tim Keller calls it "sanctification on the spot." The main way that preaching changes us is not by giving us points of application to take away from the sermon and tackle as to-dos for the coming week. Rather, as we hear with faith and behold the glory of Christ in our souls, we are "being transformed into the same image from one degree of glory to another" (2 Cor. 3:18).

This is why it is so essential that preaching be preoccupied not with the preacher or the listeners, but with Jesus. Only in perceiving him is there true power for change. Only through him and his gospel is our faith strengthened and renewed. And only in knowing and enjoying him is our soul truly satisfied.

4. To Be Equipped

Though equipping is not the main note to strike, it is a great benefit of faithful preaching. God gave "the shepherds and teachers, to equip the saints for the work of ministry, for building up the body of Christ" (Eph. 4:11–12). An important aspect of corporate worship is the building up of the church. "Strive to excel in building up the church" (1 Cor. 14:12). "Let all things be done for building up" (1 Cor. 14:26).

Because good preaching is faithful to the Bible, and the Bible is the most important source for building up the church and equipping the saints for ministry, good preaching will equip. It is not the focus, but it is a great effect.

5. To Encounter Jesus

Finally, and most importantly, the chief benefit of faithful preaching is encountering Jesus himself, and enjoying him, through hearing and receiving his word. As Martin Luther said, "To preach the gospel is nothing else than Christ's coming to us or bringing us to him."[5]

Good preaching helps us not only to forget ourselves, but to turn our gaze to the God-man, who is the only one who can satisfy our souls. In faithful preaching, we meet Jesus, and his presence is mediated to us through his word. The highest grace of preaching is encountering Christ, to know and adore him and enjoy him as our greatest treasure.

Such will significantly change our perspective and experience of preaching. What if you came to worship next time not looking merely to hear some preacher, but to encounter Jesus?

---

[5] Cited in John C. Clark and Marcus Peter Johnson, *The Incarnation of God* (Wheaton, IL: Crossway, 2015), 192.

Chapter 16

Wash in the Waters Again

———

Visible words. That was the Protestant term for baptism and the Lord's Supper in the days following the Reformation. In complement to the spoken words of gospel preaching, these twin rhythms of the gathered church are *dramatizations* of the grace of God. These "visible words" rehearse for us the center of our faith through the God-given images and actions of washing, eating, and drinking. They engage not only our ears, but all five senses—sound, sight, touch, smell, and taste. Alongside preaching, they reveal to us again and again the heart of the gospel we profess and aim to echo in our lives. They are enacted "signs," pointing to realities beyond themselves.

But these ordinances are not just signs, but "seals." They confirm to us not just that God has done something salvific for mankind in general, but that his saving grace has come to me in particular. The gospel is not only true for the world, but specifically *for me.* And when a Bible-believing, gospel-cherishing church offers the seal to me, because they consider my faith sincere, it can be a great grounds of assurance that I myself am included in the rescued people of Christ.

In this way, baptism and the Lord's Supper serve to mark us out as the church, distinct from the unbelieving world, and are part of what it means for the new covenant to be a *covenant*—with acts of both initiation and ongoing fellowship, both inauguration and renewal.

The Sacraments as Means of Grace

As theologian John Frame notes, the ordinances are not just signs and seals, but (like preaching) serve to bring God's presence near to his people.[1] Paul says in 1 Corinthians 10:16 that the bread and the cup are "a participation" in the body and blood of Jesus. They renew and strengthen our sense of being united by faith to the risen Christ. Like the other means of grace, they are not automatic, but operate through the power of the Holy Spirit *by faith*. Those who participate in faith grow in grace—as we do under the preaching of God's word— while those who engage without faith invite judgment (1 Cor. 11:27–30).[2]

These practices are not, as some have taught since the Reformation, *just* signs or *mere* symbols—nor do they "work" apart from faith, as major branches of the church have maintained. Rather, the two ordinances are means of God's grace: Christ-instituted channels of God's power, delivered by God's Spirit, dependent on Christian *faith* in the participants, given for the corporate context of the gathered church.

---

[1] Frame, *Systematic Theology* (Phillipsburg, NJ: P&R, 2013), 1060.

[2] I am a believer baptist (that's lowercase on purpose), and I find this truth to be cause for keeping those without a credible profession of faith from participating in the sacraments. Not only would I withhold the Lord's Supper to someone not confessing faith in Jesus, but baptism as well. However, the debate between evangelicals who baptize only professing believers (credobaptists) and those who also baptize the infants of believers (paedobaptists) is longstanding, and I have no delusions of ending it here. I find that many of the benefits of baptism as a means of grace are relevant both to credobaptists and paedobaptists, especially, as we will discuss below, with regards to "improving" one's baptism. However, I should note that having a conscious experience of one's baptism, and being able to remember that baptism, is not only essential in experiencing one's own baptism as a means of grace, but also a great advantage in seeking to "improve" one's baptism through watching in faith at the baptism of others. More on this below.

For many, the Lord's Supper is more manifestly an ongoing means of grace (we'll turn to the Table in the next chapter), but what about baptism?

Grace in the Water

Baptism marks new-covenant initiation. It is to be applied just once, to a believer deemed by a local congregation to have a credible profession of faith, as entrance into the full fellowship of the visible church. The gospel drama experienced, and on display, in baptism corresponds to the graces of conversion in the Christian life in first embracing the gospel—initial forgiveness and cleansing from sin, faith and repentance, the new life of the new birth, all and more in union with Christ (Rom. 6:3–5).

Baptism is not only obedience to Christ's command, and a living testimony of the candidate's faith in Jesus to all witnesses, but it also serves as a means of joy to the one being baptized. Not only is it a valuable confirmation from the visible church that we are born again, but it is a unique, one-time experience of the grace of the gospel dramatized for the one in the water, as we're symbolically buried with Jesus in death and raised to walk in newness of life (Rom. 6:4).

Improve Your Baptism

Baptism isn't a means of grace only to the one-time candidate, but also to all believers looking on with faith. This is important to the Christian, but something we often miss. The Westminster Larger Catechism (question 167) calls it "improving our baptism." Its dense statement rewards a slow read:

> The needful but much neglected duty of improving our baptism, is to be performed by us all our life long, especially in the time of temptation, and when we are present at the

administration of it to others; by serious and thankful consideration of the nature of it, and of the ends for which Christ instituted it, the privileges and benefits conferred and sealed thereby, and our solemn vow made therein; by being humbled for our sinful defilement, our falling short of, and walking contrary to, the grace of baptism, and our engagements; by growing up to assurance of pardon of sin, and of all other blessings sealed to us in that sacrament; by drawing strength from the death and resurrection of Christ, into whom we are baptized, for the mortifying of sin, and quickening of grace; and by endeavoring to live by faith, to have our conversation in holiness and righteousness, as those that have therein given up their names to Christ; and to walk in brotherly love, as being baptized by the same Spirit into one body.

That's one long, complicated sentence, but the short of it is this: Baptism is not only a blessing to us on that one memorable occasion when we were the new believer in the water. It also becomes a rehearsing of the gospel for the observer and a means of grace throughout our Christian lives as we watch, with faith, the baptisms of others and renew in our souls the riches of the reality of our identity in Christ pictured in our baptism (Rom. 6:3–4; Gal. 3:27; Col. 2:12). Wayne Grudem writes,

> Where there is genuine faith on the part of the person being baptized, and where the faith of the church that watches the baptism is stirred up and encouraged by this ceremony, then the Holy Spirit certainly does work through baptism, and it becomes a "means of grace" through which the Holy Spirit brings blessing to the person being baptized and to the church as well.[3]

---

[3] *Systematic Theology: An Introduction to Biblical Doctrine* (Grand Rapids, MI: Zondervan, 1995), 954.

Watch in Faith, Wash Your Soul

So, when your church stirs the waters, don't twiddle your thumbs waiting out this inconvenience for the remainder of the service that follows. You need not be rebaptized to experience again the grace of this drama.

Rather, with the eyes of faith, watch the gospel on display in the waters. See the preaching of Christ's sacrifice pictured for you, and hear the music of your own new life in the burying of the believer and their resurrection in Jesus. Keep your eye on the waters, and the witness. Watch in faith, and wash your soul again in the good news of being joined to Jesus.

Chapter 17

Grow in Grace at the Table

═════

The Lord's Supper is an extraordinary meal. To be sure, it is simply an ordinary means of God's grace to his church, and it is simply ordinary bread and wine. Yet as eating and drinking go, it can be an unusually powerful experience.

Along with baptism, the Supper is one of Jesus's two specially instituted sacraments for the signifying, sealing, and strengthening of his new-covenant people. Call them *ordinances* if you please. The true issue is not the term, but what we mean by it, and whether we handle these twin means of God's grace as Jesus means, to guide and shape the life of the church in her new covenant with the Bridegroom.

As we have said again and again, the means of grace are the various channels God has appointed for regularly supplying his church with spiritual power. The key principles of the means of grace are Jesus's voice (word), his ear (prayer), and his body (church). The various disciplines and practices, then—our habits of grace—are ways of *hearing him (his word), and responding (in prayer) to him, in the context of his people (the church).*

Shaped and supported by these principles, a thousand practical flowers grow in the life of the new-covenant community. But few, if any, other practices bring together all three principles of grace like the preaching of God's word, and the celebration of the sacraments, in the context of corporate worship. Here, then, are four aspects of the Supper to consider in seeing it as a means of grace.

The Gravity: Blessing or Judgment

One of the first things to note is that the Supper is not to be taken lightly. Handling the elements "in an unworthy manner" is the reason Paul gives the Corinthians for "why many of you are weak and ill, and some have died" (1 Cor. 11:27–30).

Great things are at stake when the church gathers at the Table of her Lord. Blessing and judgment are in the balance. As with preaching, and the other means of grace, there is no neutrality. Our gospel is "the aroma of Christ to God among those who are being saved and among those who are perishing, to one a fragrance from death to death, to the other a fragrance from life to life" (2 Cor. 2:15–16). So also the "visible sermon" of the Supper leads from life to life, or death to death. The Table will not leave us unaffected, but either closer to our Savior or more callous to him. This leads to a second aspect.

The Past: Rehearsing the Gospel

When instituting the Supper, Jesus instructed his disciples, "Do this in remembrance of me" (Luke 22:19), and Paul twice applies the phrase "in remembrance of me" in his instructions to the church (1 Cor. 11:24–25).

The Lord's Supper is no less than a memorial meal that draws us back to the cutting of the covenant at Calvary in Christ's self-giving sacrifice for us. With baptism and marriage and a good Christian funeral, the Table gives the life of the church a formal rhythm of remembering and rehearsing that which is of first importance (1 Cor. 15:3), the gospel of Christ's saving work for us. It helps embed gospel-centrality into the company of the redeemed.[1]

Like baptism, the Supper gives us a divinely authorized dramatization of the gospel, as the Christian receives spiritually—through physical taste, sight, smell, and touch—the pierced body and shed blood of Jesus for sinners. The Table is an act of new-covenant renewal, a repeated rite of continuing fellowship and ongoing perseverance in our embrace of the gospel. It helps us "hold fast to the word" (1 Cor. 15:2) and "continue in the faith, stable and steadfast, not shifting from the hope of the gospel" (Col. 1:23).

The Present: Proclaiming His Death

So the Table is more than simply a memorial. In this rich recollection of Jesus's sacrifice, and the taking of the elements in faith, comes a present proclamation of his death and its meaning. "As often as you eat this bread and drink the cup, you *proclaim the Lord's death* until he comes" (1 Cor. 11:26). This visible sermon, like audible preaching, is "able to strengthen you" according to the gospel (Rom. 16:25) as a means of grace to those who watch and partake in faith. Those who participate without faith are "guilty concerning the body and blood of the Lord" (1 Cor. 11:27) and eat and drink judgment on themselves (1 Cor. 11:29), while "those who eat and drink in a worthy manner partake of Christ's body and blood, not physically, but

---

[1] Weddings and funerals can be seen as means of God's grace when approached in faith. In the wedding, we see the depicting of the covenant between Christ and his church. In a funeral, the death of the person being honored reminds us not only that life is a vapor (James 4:14), but also of our own finitude, the effects of sin, and the coming final victory of Christ over sin and death (1 Cor. 15:54–58). The Protestant church (rightly) has not considered them sacraments or ordinances; however, they are helpful reminders of the gospel and can serve as means of grace for those with faith.

spiritually, in that, by faith, they are nourished with the benefits he obtained through his death, and thus grow in grace."[2]

In this way, the Lord's Supper is a powerful pathway for deepening and sustaining the Christian life. "Participation in the Lord's Supper," writes Wayne Grudem, is

> very clearly a means of grace which the Holy Spirit uses to bring blessing to his church. . . . We should expect that the Lord would give spiritual blessing as we participate in the Lord's Supper in faith and in obedience to the directions laid down in Scripture, and in this way it is a "means of grace" which the Holy Spirit uses to convey blessing to us. . . .
>
> There is a spiritual union among believers and with the Lord that is strengthened and solidified at the Lord's Supper, and it is not to be taken lightly.[3]

The Future: Awaiting the Feast

As the Westminster Confession of Faith states, the Table, received in faith, is for our "spiritual nourishment and growth."[4] It not only strengthens our union with Jesus, but also our communion with fellow believers in Christ. As we come together to the Supper to feed spiritually on Christ (John 6:53–58), he draws us closer not only to himself, but also to others in the body (1 Cor. 10:17).

Here at the Table, we hear Jesus's voice, have our Savior's ear, and commune with him and others in his body. We receive afresh his gospel, respond in faith, and knit our hearts together in the bread and cup we share. And in doing so, we look not only to the past and remember what he's done, and not only

[2] Desiring God Affirmation of Faith, 12.4, available at http://www.desiringgod.org/about /affirmation-of-faith.
[3] *Systematic Theology: An Introduction to Biblical Doctrine* (Grand Rapids, MI: Zondervan, 1995), 954–55.
[4] WCF, 29.1.

to the present and our growing union with him, but also to the future and the full feast to come at his great wedding supper (Rev. 19:9). "As often as you eat this bread and drink the cup, you proclaim the Lord's death *until he comes*" (1 Cor. 11:26).

"We eat only little bits of bread and drink little cups of wine," says John Frame, "for we know that our fellowship with Christ in this life cannot begin to compare with the glory that awaits us in him."[5]

---

[5] *Systematic Theology* (Phillipsburg, NJ: P&R, 2013), 1069.

Chapter 18

Embrace the Blessing of Rebuke

═══════

One of the most loving things we can do for each other in the church is tell each other when we're wrong. Call it correction, reproof, or rebuke—Paul uses all three terms in just four verses in 2 Timothy 3:16–4:2—but don't miss what makes it distinctively Christian, and a gift to our souls: *It is a great act of love.* The kind of rebuke that the Scriptures commend is the kind intended to stop us from continuing on a destructive path.

There are at least two participants in a rebuke that serves our souls as a means of God's grace. One is the giver; the other receives. In this chapter, we focus first on receiving a rebuke from a brother as a grace from God; then we look at what it means to be a means of God's grace in giving rebuke in humility and love.

Watershed of Wisdom

Reproof is a fork in the road for a sinful soul. Will we cringe at correction like a curse, or embrace rebuke as a blessing?

One of the great themes in Proverbs is that those who embrace rebuke are wise and walk the path of life, while those who despise reproof find themselves to be fools careening toward death.

The proverbial warnings against dismissing brotherly correction are staggering. The one who rejects reproof leads others astray (Prov. 10:17), is stupid (12:1) and a fool (15:5), and despises himself (15:32). "Whoever hates reproof will die" (15:10), and "poverty and disgrace come to him" (13:18).

But just as astounding are the promises of blessing to those who embrace rebuke. "Whoever heeds reproof is honored" (Prov. 13:18) and prudent (15:5). "He who listens to reproof gains intelligence" (15:32), loves knowledge (12:1), will dwell among the wise (15:31), and is on the path of life (10:17)—because "the rod and reproof give wisdom" (29:15) and "the reproofs of discipline are the way of life" (6:23).

To the one who embraces rebuke, God says, "I will pour out my spirit to you" (Prov. 1:23), but to the one who despises it, "I will laugh at your calamity" (1:25–26). It will be said of those who reject correction, "They shall eat the fruit of their way, and have their fill of their own devices" (1:30–31), and it's only a matter of time until they themselves will say, "I am at the brink of utter ruin" (5:12–14).

And when ruin comes for the fool who resists reproof, it will be sudden and devastating: "He who is often reproved, yet stiffens his neck, will suddenly be broken beyond healing" (Prov. 29:1).

Open the Gift

The wise recognize rebuke as a gift of gold (Prov. 25:12). It is kindness, and a token of love. "Let a righteous man strike me—it is a kindness; let him rebuke me—it is oil for my head; let my head not refuse it" (Ps. 141:5).

Typically it is easier for others in our lives not to say anything but just let us go merrily on our way down the path of folly and death. But reproof is an act of love, a willingness to own that awkward moment, and perhaps having your counsel thrown back in your face, for the risk of doing someone good. When a spouse or friend or family member or associate rises to the level of such love, we should be profoundly thankful.

Hear God's Voice in Your Brother's

Those of us who have in Christ "all the treasures of wisdom and knowledge" (Col. 2:3), and are in our right mind, will want to "listen to advice and accept instruction, that [we] may gain wisdom in the future" (Prov. 19:20). We'll not just suffer a brother or sister speaking into our lives on rare occasion, but invite them to do so—and when they do, embrace it as a blessing. Even when it's a rebuke poorly delivered, and the timing and tone are poor, and the motivation seems suspect, we'll want to ransack it for every grain of truth, and then repent and thank God for the grace of having people in our lives who love us enough to say something hard.

Not wanting to "despise the Lord's discipline or be weary of his reproof" (Prov. 3:11), we'll ask, *how is it that God's reproof most often comes to me?* Answer: in reproof from a brother or sister in Christ. We'll beware resisting the reproof of a fellow in Jesus, especially when it's echoed in multiple voices, knowing that likely we would be resisting the very reproof of God.

When a brother or sister in Christ goes to the inconvenience to have the unpleasant conversation that brings correction into our lives, we should be floored with thanksgiving. "The Lord reproves him whom he loves" (Prov. 3:12). Count it as love from your brother, and as God's channel of his love for you.

Easier Said Than Done

But all of that, of course, is much easier said than done. Deep down in the caverns of our remaining sin, where we can be most callous to true grace in its varied forms, we don't want to hear correction. Something rebellious in us recoils.

When we hear that "all Scripture is breathed out by God and profitable," it's natural to be more excited about it being "for teaching" and "for training in righteousness" than "for reproof" and "for correction" (2 Tim. 3:16). That's too personal. That touches a nerve.

And forces from without don't make it any easier. It shouldn't surprise us that the societal air we breathe is hostile to correction and reproof, even in its most gentle and loving varieties. If humanity isn't recognized to be depraved in nature and sinful in practice, then rebuke is no longer a lifesaver but an annoyance, even an offense. But if we do acknowledge that we are flawed, selfish, and arrogant and regularly sin with our words and actions, then we will learn to see a brother's rebuke for the tremendous grace that it is.

Unlock the Power

But however much receiving reproof goes against our native instincts or catches us off our gospel guard in the moment, we have this great hope to grow into: The love of Christ for us is our key to unlock the power of rebuke. With him in view, the one "who loved me and gave himself for me" (Gal. 2:20), no longer must reproof be an assault on our very foundations and deep sense of worth, but it becomes a fresh opportunity for growth and greater joy.

It is another grace of the gospel that by the Spirit we can grow skin thick enough to hear any reproof as a pathway to yet even more grace. It is the gospel that gives us the wherewithal for truly leaning into rebuke and receiving its bounty. Only in Jesus can we find our identity not in being without fault, but in being shown love by God when we're still sinners, chock-full of faults (Rom. 5:8). With such a Savior to steady our feet, we can embrace rebuke for the blessing that it is.

Give the Blessing of Rebuke

Rebuke is a blessing that takes two. Love compels us not only to want to receive a rebuke with a gospel identity, but also to give others the gift. One of the most loving things we can do for others is tell them when they're in the wrong.

While it's tough enough to embrace the blessing of rebuke when you find yourself the recipient of some corrective word, it can be even more difficult initiating that awkward moment, and carrying through, on loving someone enough to call them out. "If it is hard to accept a rebuke, even a private one," says D. A. Carson, "it is harder still to administer one in loving humility."[1]

But however difficult it may be, if we really believe that we all are sinners and that unchecked sin leads to pain and misery and eternal destruction, love will constrain us to give the gift of loving reproof. Here, then, in the spirit of seeking to provide reproof in "loving humility," are seven steps toward correction that is truly Christian.

1. Check Your Own Heart First

The words of Jesus are a good place to begin. Often the subtle expressions of sin we see in others catch our eye because they find resonance in our own hearts. Our indwelling pride is quick to alert us to pride in others. Unconquered greed in our hearts

---

[1] *Matthew*, rev. ed. The Expositor's Bible Commentary (Grand Rapids, MI: Zondervan, 2010), 456.

notices others' love for possessions. A slip of the tongue to which we're also prone grabs our attention in someone else.

So, a first step when encountering sin in others is following Jesus's clear directive: "First take the log out of your own eye, and then you will see clearly to take the speck out of your brother's eye" (Matt. 7:5). And remember the charge of Galatians 6:1 when helping to restore a brother: "Keep watch on yourself, lest you too be tempted."

What, then, do we do when we find the speck of someone else's sin in us as well? Does it mean that the opportunity to help a brother has passed, because we have enough work to do on ourselves? It may. But hopefully not. Before approaching him about his sin, renew your own repentance in your tendencies to the same temptation, and then come to your brother with fresh humility and empathy, as a fellow combatant of that sin.

2. Seek to Sympathize

Whether you've "been there" and can empathize with the other person's specific sin or not, pray for sympathy and seek to mind what we might consider the Golden Rule of Rebuke: "Whatever you wish that others would do to you, do also to them" (Matt. 7:12).

On the one hand, this should confirm that when we observe something in a brother that warrants correction, the loving thing is not just to let it slide but bring it to his attention. Isn't that what the most sanctified part of you would want as well? And, on the other hand, that leads us to do so with a certain posture and demeanor—what Carson calls "loving humility."

As much as you're able, put yourself in their shoes, and consider how to remind them of foundational gospel truths as you seek to open their eyes to some further reality relating to their remaining sin. Consider the manner in which you'd want to be approached with such an observation, and give extra effort to make sure it comes off as a word of brotherly correction, not condemnation. "Bear one another's burdens, and so fulfill the law of Christ" (Gal. 6:2).

3. Pray for Restoration

Having checked your own eye and sought sympathy, pray for others before confronting them. Pray about the moment you approach them, that you would give your word of correction sufficient gospel preface, that they would receive your loving reproof, and that if they resist in the moment, God would soon soften their heart to the degree that your observation is true. Also pray for loving courage to gently hold your ground and not immediately backtrack if they snap back or their inner lawyer immediately objects.

Pray and speak toward restoration, not merely righting wrongs and appeasing your own judicial sentiment. Whether it's the formal process of Matthew 18:15–17 in response to some egregious error or misstep, or the informal everyday exhortations of Hebrews 3:12–13 for life in community, all biblical correction aims at restoration (Luke 17:3–4; 2 Thess. 3:14–15; James 5:19–20).

4. Be Quick

Pray for the other person's restoration, but don't wait there too long on your knees. Hebrews encourages us to be quick and regular—"every day." Don't let manifestly sinful patterns fester. If possible, don't even let the sun go down.

> Take care, brothers, lest there be in any of you an evil, unbelieving heart, leading you to fall away from the living God. But exhort one another *every day*, as long as it is called "today," that none of you may be hardened by the deceitfulness of sin. (Heb. 3:12–13)

Providing a corrective word in loving humility is not only for words and actions that are dead wrong or borderline blasphemous, but when we become aware of some seeming trajectory of evil or deception. The ideal is that we live in such honest and regular community—and speak without delay and receive it with gospel-conditioned thick skin—that mild, gentle words of rebuke and correction are commonplace, that sin is regularly nipped in the bud rather than given time and space to grow into the tall nasty weed it will become.

5. BE KIND

What makes a corrective word to be truly Christian is not only explicit reminders of gospel truths, but also a tone and demeanor that matches our Master. There is a place for gravity and severity in response to clear callousness of heart, but most often, in the kind of regular correction we provide for each other in community, it is the gentle pattern of "the Lord's servant" that sets our course:

> The Lord's servant must not be quarrelsome but *kind to everyone*, able to teach, patiently enduring evil, *correcting his opponents with gentleness*. God may perhaps grant them repentance leading to a knowledge of the truth, and they may come to their senses and escape from the snare of the devil, after being captured by him to do his will. (2 Tim. 2:24–26)

In one sense, any righteous rebuke is a kindness. "Let a righteous man strike me—it is a kindness; let him rebuke me—it is oil for my head; let my head not refuse it" (Ps. 141:5). But it is all the more a gift when such a kindness is given kindly. And if we are to correct an opponent with gentleness (2 Tim. 2:25), how much more a friend.

As much as vestiges of sin in us would make our hands harsh with fellow sinners, the Spirit works another pattern in us as we walk in light of the gospel. "Brothers, if anyone is caught in any transgression, you who are spiritual should restore him in a spirit of gentleness" (Gal. 6:1).

6. Be Clear and Specific

But your kindness may send the wrong message if it is not matched with clarity. When we've checked our own heart, sought sympathy, prayed for restoration, and have been quick and kind in addressing the sin, we now are empowered to be frank and direct, without needing to tiptoe around what's really caught our attention.

Before approaching someone with a corrective word, get it clear in your own mind what you're observing and how it may be harmful. You may even want to scratch a few key words or phrases or sentences on paper to make sure it's objective enough to communicate and not too mired in your own subjective sense. Have specific examples ready. Pray for, and then take up, the apostle's love of clarity and "open statement of the truth" (2 Cor. 4:2). His prayer in Colossians 4:4 is about transparency in speaking the gospel, but it relates as well to correcting our brother: "That I may make it clear, which is how I ought to speak."

7. Follow Up

Finally, plan some way to follow up. If they receive it well, follow up with a note or call or conversation, and commend that evidence of grace in their life. If they don't respond well, follow up with some further expression of love for them, perhaps a reminder that you have nothing to gain but their good, that you're happy to be wrong if the correction was pretty subjective, and that you're praying for them as they consider your observation.

Providing regular, gracious words of correction can seem like such a small thing in community life. It's so easy just to let little sins go and mind your own business. But the long-term effect of such active grace, administered in loving humility, can have eternal implications. "My brothers, if anyone among you wanders from the truth and someone brings him back, let him know that whoever brings back a sinner from his wandering will save his soul from death and will cover a multitude of sins" (James 5:19–20).

Part 4

CODA

Chapter 19

The Commission

———

We said at the beginning there wouldn't be room in a book of this size for an exhaustive treatment of the means of grace and the many good habits we can cultivate around them. There is so much more to be said at the level of principle and theology, not to mention countless more specifics and creative ideas we could get into for everyday practice. I leave those to other authors, and better yet, to your own ingenuity and trial and error, and others in your life and community. But before parting, it will be helpful to briefly touch on three more practically oriented topics that are closely related to the means of grace.

Many have considered evangelism and stewardship (of both time and money) to be spiritual disciplines. There certainly are elements here that involve discipline, and there are biblical principles and promises that would rightly lead us to think of these as means of grace in some real sense. However, I find it most helpful to treat mission, time, and money together as disciplines and pursuits that are first and foremost effects of our regular hearing of God's word, having his ear, and belonging to his body. Receiving God's ongoing grace for our souls sustains us, inspires us, and empowers us for evangelism and stewardship. And when we talk about the clock (chap. 21) and the dollar (chap. 20), it may be most helpful to do so within the framework of the Great Commission.

Mission as a Means of Grace

We will only go so deep with Jesus until we start yearning to reach out. When our life in him is healthy and vibrant, we not only ache to keep sinking our roots down deep in him, but we also want to stretch out our branches and extend his goodness to others.

But not only does going deep with Jesus soon lead us to reach out to others, but also reaching out leads us deeper with him. In other words, getting on board with Jesus's mission to disciple the nations may be the very thing he uses to push through your spiritual lethargy and jump-start your stalled sanctification. One veteran pastor writes,

> Often I meet Christians who are in spiritual malaise, holding on to their faith but not advancing it much. Bible study has become a chore; prayer is a dry routine. The miracle of their own conversion, once recounted with great passion, is now a distant, fading memory. And going to church is—well, it's something they just do. Mechanically and halfheartedly, these people trudge along through the drudgery of quarantined Christianity.
>
> But when these lethargic believers break out of spiritual isolation and meet some spiritual seekers, something incredible starts to happen. As they experience the high-stakes conversations that tend to happen with unchurched people, they begin to notice a sort of inner renewal taking place. Areas long ignored suddenly come alive with fresh significance. . . . Isn't it incredible how elevating

our efforts to reach others can be a catalyst for personal growth?[1]

Living on mission is not only an effect of God's grace coming to us through the channels of his word, prayer, and fellowship, but it also may become a means of his grace to us in the whole of the Christian life.

Disciplemaking as a Means of Grace

Disciplemaking is the process in which a maturing believer invests himself, for a particular period of time, in one or just a few younger believers, in order to help their growth in the faith—including helping them also to invest in others who will invest in others. Such was the lion's share of Jesus's ministry, from the time he called to only twelve, "Follow me, and I will make you fishers of men" (Matt. 4:19), until he sent them out, "Go therefore and make disciples of all nations" (Matt. 28:19).

It's not surprising that we typically think of disciplemaking as one-sided. The "older," more mature Christian is giving of his time and energy to intentionally invest in a younger believer. The discipler's own enjoyment of the means of grace (word, prayer, and fellowship) serves to fuel him spiritually for pouring out into others. However, disciplemaking is the very stuff of Christian fellowship, and every believer, indwelt by God's Spirit, can be a channel of God's grace to anyone else. This means good disciplemaking is always a two-way street. The "disciple" and the "discipler" are most fundamentally disciples of Jesus. And so, as Stephen Smallman says, "Our involvement in making disciples will be one of the most significant things we can do for our own growth as disciples."[2] It's like any subject; we get it better ourselves when we teach it to others.

---

[1] Bill Hybels, *Becoming a Contagious Christian* (Grand Rapids, MI: Zondervan, 1996), 30, 32.
[2] *The Walk: Steps for New and Renewed Followers of Jesus* (Phillipsburg, NJ: P&R, 2009), 211.

Making disciples is a great means of God's ongoing grace in the life of the one doing the discipling. Here are four ways, among many.

1. Disciplemaking Shows Us Our Smallness and God's Bigness

Actively making disciples helps us see our lives in better proportion—not with ourselves at the center, doing the big things, but situated happily on the periphery, doing our small part in a big and glorious God-sized plan. It is astonishing that Jesus says "the nations." *Disciple the nations.* The vision is huge—as big as it could be. And yet our part is small.

One memorable refrain I've heard over and over again in Campus Outreach circles is "think big, start small, go deep." Think big: God's global glory, among all the nations. Start small: focus on a few, like Jesus did. Go deep: invest at depth in those few, so deeply that they will be equipped and prepared to do the same in the lives of others.

Disciplemaking is as massive as the Great Commission and as minute and seemingly menial as everyday life. The Christian life not only connects our little lives with God's global purposes, but it also translates the bigness of the mission into the smallness of our daily actions. Disciplemaking is a major way—and the only way expressly in the Commission—in which our minor, local lives connect to God's major, global plan.

Here there is a place for the Christian's almost heroic, big-picture, world-changing impulse. But such vision is fleshed out in the uncelebrated, unsexy normalcy of everyday life. *Think big, start small, go deep.* Envision big, global, many. Act small, local, few. As Robert Coleman writes, "One cannot transform a world except as individuals in the world are transformed."[3]

---

[3] *The Master Plan of Evangelism* (Grand Rapids, MI: Revell, 1993), 23.

2. Disciplemaking Challenges Us to Be Holistic Christians

As we invest in younger believers toward their balanced, overall spiritual growth, we ourselves are reminded of, and encouraged toward, holistic health in the faith.

Good disciplemaking requires both intentionality and relationality. It means being strategic *and* being social. Most of us are bent one way or the other. We're naturally relational, but lacking in intentionality. Or we find it easy to be intentional, but not relational. We typically tip (or sometimes lean) one way or the other as we begin the disciplemaking process.

But tipping and leaning won't cover the full picture of what life-on-life disciplemaking requires. It's not just friend-to-friend, and it's not just teacher-to-student. It's both. There is the sharing of ordinary life (relationship) and seeking to initiate and make the most of teachable moments (intentionality). There are the long walks through Galilee and the sermons on the mount. Disciplemaking is both organic and engineered, relational and intentional, with shared context and shared content, quality and quantity time.

3. Disciplemaking Makes Us More Aware of Our Sin

Disciplemaking is more than mere truth-speaking; it is also life-sharing, as Paul writes to the Thessalonians: "We were ready to share with you not only the gospel of God but also our own selves" (1 Thess. 2:8). Whenever Paul says "not only the gospel," sit up and take notice. This is important stuff.

Sharing your own self with someone means getting close—not just sharing information, but sharing life, sharing space. And the closer sinners get, the more sin comes out (which is why marriage can be such a matrix for sanctification as two sinners get increasingly close).

In good disciplemaking we are able to demonstrate for the ones we're investing in something that Jesus's disciples never saw in him: how to repent. Those who are looking to our lives and seeking to imitate our faith need to see us be honest and forthright about our sins, hear our confessions, witness our repentance, and watch us earnestly pursue change.

To get more specific, disciplemaking requires that we die to selfishness—selfishness with our time and with our space. To get even more specific, it means dying to much of our precious privacy. Most of us do life alone so much more than is necessary. But in disciplemaking, we ask, How can we live the Christian life *together*? How can I give this younger Christian access to my real life, not some triumphal facade I put on once a week? It marks the death to much of our privacy. We bring that one or few in whom we are investing into the process and mess of our sanctification as we enter into theirs.

We have to "be with them" (Mark 3:14) to have the kind of effect Jesus had on his men: "Now when they saw the boldness of Peter and John, and perceived that they were uneducated, common men, they were astonished. And they recognized that they had been with Jesus" (Acts 4:13). And as we do so, new manifestations of sin will be exposed in us, and we'll find ourselves all the more in need of God's ongoing grace.

4. Disciplemaking Teaches Us to Lean Heavier on Jesus

Disciplemaking is often messy, difficult work. You will see your weaknesses and failures and inadequacies like never before, and with God's help, it will teach you all the more to lean on Jesus.

Good disciplers must learn, in reliance on the Spirit, how to deal well with failure. And the Christian way to deal well with failure is take it to the cross.

As simple as disciplemaking may sound, it will not be easy, and if you are honest with yourself, it will not be without failure. Failures in our love. Failures in initiating. Failures to share the gospel with clarity and boldness. Failures to share our own selves because of selfishness. Failures to follow through, and sufficiently equip, and pray without ceasing, and walk in patience.

Disciplemaking hems us in, exposes our failures, and teaches us to draw our daily strength not from ourselves but from Jesus and the gospel, which are the essence of disciplemaking. The gospel is the baton to be passed. This is the content, "the deposit" (1 Tim. 6:20; 2 Tim. 1:14) passed from one spiritual generation to the next. This is the treasure in us we work to build into other jars of clay (2 Cor. 4:7).

We disciple not to clone ourselves, not to reproduce our idiosyncrasies and personal hobbyhorses. Rather, we make disciples to pass on the gospel. We don't center on ourselves, but on Jesus, who is not only the great model but also the content of disciplemaking. We baptize in Jesus's name, not ours. And we teach others to observe everything that he has commanded, not what we personally would advise.

But Jesus and his gospel are not only the main content of disciplemaking. Jesus is also the flawed and failing discipler's Great Comfort, who frees us from having to be the perfect discipler. There has already been one—and he was perfect all the way from the shores of Galilee to the cross of Calvary, where he took our sins and failures. We need not imitate his perfection in disciplemaking. We cannot.

But we can take great comfort that in him our failures are covered, and that the sovereign One who promises to build his church and be with us always as we carry out his Commission loves to sanctify half-baked, substandard disciplemaking and make himself look good by showing himself, not the underling discipler, to be the great power source behind it.

Chapter 20

The Dollar

━━━

For the Christian, the issue is not just *that* we give, but *how*. "God loves a cheerful giver" (2 Cor. 9:7). And giving gladly rests on the great *why* of Christian generosity: that Christ himself—our Savior, Lord, and greatest treasure—demonstrated the ultimate in generosity in coming to buy us back. "Though he was rich, yet for your sake he became poor, so that you by his poverty might become rich" (2 Cor. 8:9). If Jesus is in us, then increasingly such an open-handed tendency will be in us as well.

One of the effects of the gospel going deeper into our souls is that it frees our fingers to loosen their grasp on our goods. Generosity is one of the great evidences of truly being a Christian. Not only is it Jesus himself who speaks most often, and warns us more severely, about the danger of greed, but he is also the one who so strongly appeals to our joy and says, "It is more blessed to give than to receive" (Acts 20:35).

Here are five truths to rehearse for spending and giving in the service of loving others and advancing the mission.

1. Money Is a Tool

Money itself is not evil. It is not wealth *per se* that is sinful, but the "desire to be rich" (1 Tim. 6:9). It is not money, but "the *love* of money" that is "a root of all kinds of evils" (1 Tim. 6:10), from which we should keep our lives free (Heb. 13:5). It is "this craving" (1 Tim. 6:10) in our sinful hearts which is so dangerous.

With all the strong warnings in the Bible about how we orient toward money (like the condemnation of luxury and self-indulgence in James 5:1–6), it can be easy to forget that the problem isn't money, but our hearts. Finances, salaries, and budgets are an important part of the world our Lord created and entered into as a creature, with all its limitations of space, time, and finitude.

When Jesus's opponents asked about taxes to Caesar, he didn't decry the evils of money, but relativized its role in relation to God (Matt. 22:21). When they came looking for his temple tax, he made (miraculous) provision for both himself and Peter (Matt. 17:27). He even commended, in the face of Judas's objections, Mary's lavish display of love in anointing his feet with expensive ointment (worth more than a year's wages). Jesus would even have us go so far as to "make friends for yourselves by means of unrighteous wealth, so that when it fails they may receive you into the eternal dwellings" (Luke 16:9). In other words, money is a tool that can be used for long-term godward goals, not just short-term selfish purposes.

And tools are made to be used. Holding onto money will not satisfy our souls or meet the needs of others.

2. How We Use Money Reveals Our Hearts

Matthew 6:21 holds an important reminder: "Where your treasure is, there your heart will be also." Hoarding our money says something: that we fear not having sufficient funds at some point in the future. Parsimony betrays our unbelief in the provision of our heavenly Father (Matt. 6:26) and his promise to "supply every need of yours according to his riches in glory in Christ Jesus" (Phil. 4:19).

Giving it away also speaks. It is an opportunity to show, and reinforce, the place of faith and love in our hearts. It's a chance to gladly pursue the first and second greatest commandments through our giving, and to cultivate the mind of Christ through our spending: "Let each of you look not only to his own interests, but also to the interests of others" (Phil. 2:4). It's telling that Paul would couple "lovers of money" with "lovers of self" (2 Tim. 3:2).

But the greatest test of our treasure is not whether we're willing to spend it, but whom and what we spend it on. Generosity is an occasion to look past the small joys of self-oriented spending, and pursue the greater pleasures of spending on others. And so a good instinct to develop on the threshold of significant purchases is to ask what this expenditure reveals about our heart. What desire am I trying to fulfill? Is this for private comfort, or gospel advance, or expressing love to a friend or family member?

3. Sacrifice Varies from Person to Person

But hoarding and giving aren't the only options. For most of us, the vast majority of our spending goes to meet our own needs and the needs of our families. That kind of spending is inevitable and necessary. It is a good thing. God provides us with income for those purposes. And to many of us, he gives resources beyond our needs and enables us to join him in the joy of giving to others.

This raises the question of how much is enough for "our needs." Is it simply food, clothing, and shelter in meager proportions? Where is the line between righteous and unrighteous spending on ourselves? Are there any standards to help us know how much to keep and how much to let go to others in generosity?

Augustine offers a standard in "the needs of this life," which is summarized by Rebecca DeYoung:

> . . . not just what is necessary for bare subsistence, but also what is necessary for living a life "becoming" or appropriate to human beings. The point is not to live on crusts of bread with bare walls and threadbare clothes. The point is that a fully human life is lived in a way free from being enslaved to our stuff. Our possessions are meant to serve our needs and our humanness, rather than our lives being centered around service to our possessions and our desires for them.[1]

No doubt, discerning what is, and is not, "a fully human life . . . free from being enslaved to our stuff" will vary from place to place and person to person. *"Each one must give as he has decided in his heart*, not reluctantly or under compulsion, for God loves a cheerful giver" (2 Cor. 9:7). When it comes to finances, we all do well to be critical of ourselves, rather than others—and to remind ourselves how prone we are to be easy on ourselves and hard on others.

It's difficult, and probably unwise, to prescribe particulars here, but we can create some helpful categories, and describe errors to avoid, like "being enslaved to our stuff." One thing to note is that "a fully human life" is not a static existence. God made us for rhythms and cadences, for feasting and fasting, for noise and crowds and silence and solitude. There is some help, even if minimal, in identifying and naming the extremes

---

[1] *Glittering Vices: A New Look at the Seven Deadly Sins and Their Remedies* (Grand Rapids, MI: Brazos, 2009), 106.

of sustained opulence and austerity. We need a place for both financial feasting and fasting. We should abhor the so-called "prosperity gospel," and not be snookered by stinginess masquerading as Christian stewardship, and beware that running up large credit-card debt is likely giving beyond our means.

While discerning precisely what's too little or too much from person to person is no easy task, John Piper wisely observes, "The impossibility of drawing a line between night and day doesn't mean you can't know it's midnight."[2]

A final thing to note in terms of standard is the test of sacrifice. Do you ever abstain from something you'd otherwise think of as "the needs of life" in order to give to others?

Nothing shows our hearts like sacrifice. When we are willing not only to give from our excess, but to embrace some personal loss or disadvantage for the sake of showing generosity toward others, we say loudly and clearly, even if only to our own souls, that we have a greater love than ourselves and our comforts.

4. Generosity Is a Means of Grace

Such sacrifice raises the question that has been under the surface all along in addressing the subject of giving: Is there any *reward* for generosity and sacrifice—whether we're giving Christmas presents or year-end donations or a meal to a friend or stranger—other than our own existential release and sense of joy from an act of selflessness? Is giving to others, in God's economy, a channel for our own receipt of grace from above?

While the New Testament does not promise physical rewards in this lifetime for our giving, it does teach that generosity is a means of grace for our souls, and that God stands ready to bless those who give from faith. "It is *more blessed* to give

---

[2] Collin Hansen interview with John Piper, "Piper on Pastors' Pay," The Gospel Coalition, November 6, 2013, http://www.thegospelcoalition.org/article/piper-on-pastors-pay.

than to receive" (Acts 20:35). And the promise is even stronger in 2 Corinthians 9:

- Verse 6: "Whoever sows sparingly will also reap sparingly, and whoever sows bountifully will also reap bountifully."
- Verse 8: "God is able to make all grace abound to you, so that having all sufficiency in all things at all times, you may abound in every good work."
- Verses 10–11: "He who supplies seed to the sower and bread for food will supply and multiply your seed for sowing and increase the harvest of your righteousness. You will be enriched in every way to be generous in every way, which through us will produce thanksgiving to God."

It is the grace of God that frees a soul from selfishness and empowers not just generosity, but sacrifice. And such sacrifice God will not overlook. In faith, our giving to meet others' needs becomes an occasion for more divine grace to flood our souls.

5. God Is the Most Cheerful Giver

In the end, as cheerfully as we may give, we cannot out-give the truly cheerful Giver. Willingly, he gave his own Son (John 3:16; Rom. 8:32), as he had decided in his heart, not reluctantly or under compulsion, but with joy.

And Jesus himself was willing from the heart, offering himself in his own eternal spirit (Heb. 9:14) and sacrificing the truest of riches to meet our greatest need. "You know the grace of our Lord Jesus Christ, that though he was rich, yet for your sake he became poor, so that you by his poverty might become rich" (2 Cor. 8:9).

God loves a cheerful giver because he is one, the consummate one. And every gift we give in Christ is simply an echo of what we have already received, and the immeasurable riches to come (Eph. 2:7).

Chapter 21

The Clock

===

You are always on the clock. There's no avoiding it. Every human, in every place on the planet, whatever the culture, is subject to the incessant passing of time. The sands are always falling. No matter how much we neglect it, suppress it, or stress about it, there is nothing we can do to stem the onslaught. Ignore the rush to your own peril. Or walk the path of wisdom in stewarding your short and few days as gifts from God.

The first thing to say about being intentional with our time is that Scripture commends it. Giving attention to better time management isn't a secular creation. The recent glut of business books on the topic is long preceded by the teaching of the Bible.

Not only does the apostle Paul give us the charter, "Look carefully then how you walk . . . making the best use of the time" (Eph. 5:15–16), but even a millennium and a half earlier, the Prayer of Moses asked for God's help "to number our days that we may get a heart of wisdom" (Ps. 90:12).

The Scriptures have plenty to say about stewarding our money, and it doesn't take much to see that the clock is even more precious than the dollar. As Donald S. Whitney reasons, "If people threw away their money as thoughtlessly as they throw away their time, we would think them insane. Yet time is infinitely more precious than money because money can't buy time."[1]

If the Lord Wills

But the Bible not only commends time management; it also cautions it. Yes, neglect is a frequent danger, but the opposite pitfall is nearly epidemic in our day. Whether the root sin is anxiety, selfishness, or simple pride and arrogance, the answer to neglect isn't a pendulum swing to our being consumed by our calendars. The god of time management will fail us quickly in the place of Christ and his providence and prerogatives.

James takes the lead voice in chastising, or at least sanctifying, our scheduling.

> Come now, you who say, "Today or tomorrow we will go into such and such a town and spend a year there and trade and make a profit"—yet you do not know what tomorrow will bring. What is your life? For you are a mist that appears for a little time and then vanishes. Instead you ought to say, "If the Lord wills, we will live and do this or that." As it is, you boast in your arrogance. All such boasting is evil. (James 4:13–16)

James echoes the counsel of Proverbs 27:1, "Do not boast about tomorrow, for you do not know what a day may bring." We can forecast, but we don't know what the next hour will hold, much less the next week. As much as our time may seem like our own, every clock is ultimately God's. He may carry us into old age and gray hairs (Isa. 46:4), or he may say, without

---

[1] *Spiritual Disciplines for the Christian Life*, rev. ed. (Colorado Springs: NavPress, 2014), 166–67.

warning, "Fool! This night your soul is required of you" (Luke 12:20).

The hands of the clock are ever in the hands of God. It is arrogant to plan without planning for God.

Productivity Porn

Surely, too many are negligent with their time, but we live in a day in which time management is in vogue. At least in the West, we may be more aware of the clock, and how fleeting it is, than ever before. Your local bookstore now offers more new titles on productivity and time management than philosophy and religion. "Productivity porn" has ensnared myriads in its web of ever-improving systems.[2]

Today, the experts tell us to take charge of our daily routine before someone else does, that the biggest problem we face is "reactionary workflow," and that we must vigilantly guard our sacred schedule from the invasions of others' needs and priorities.[3]

Perhaps more than ever, we need to hear from our loving Father the hard but happy reminder of 1 Corinthians 6:19–20 tailored to our planning: *Your time is not your own. You were bought with a price. So glorify me in your schedule.*

But then what? If our time is ultimately not our own, but his, how will faith direct the time we are stewarding on loan?

Faith Working through Love

One key principle in making our time management Christian is this: *Let love for others be the driver of your disciplined, intentional planning.* It is love for others that fulfills God's law (Rom.

---

[2] James Bedell, "The Trap of Productivity Porn," Medium.com, December 21, 2013, http://www.medium.com/thinking-about-thinking/the-trap-of-productivity-porn-7173d1cc6f95.

[3] For instance, *Manage Your Day-to-Day: Build Your Routing, Find Your Focus, and Sharpen Your Creative Mind*, ed. Jocelyn Glei, 99U Book Series (Las Vegas: Amazon Publishing, 2013).

13:8, 10). Sanctifying our time godward will mean spending it on others in the manifold acts of love. Good works glorify God not by meeting his needs (he doesn't have any, Acts 17:25), but through serving others. As Martin Luther so memorably said, it is not God who needs your good works, but your neighbor.

When we ask that God teach us to count our days, this is the lesson we learn time and again. One way to make it practical is to schedule the time both for proactive good in the calling God has given us and reactive good that responds to the urgent needs of others. Learning to let love inspire and drive our planning likely will mean fairly rigid blocks for our proactive labors, along with generous margin and planned flexibility to regularly meet the unplanned needs of others.

Perhaps there's a whole theology of time management just below the surface at the end of Paul's short letter to his protégé Titus. "Let our people learn to devote themselves to good works," he writes, "so as to help cases of urgent need, and not be unfruitful" (Titus 3:14). Fruitfulness (productivity) means meeting others' needs with "good works"—expenditures of our time, energy, and money in the service of love—which will be both proactive and reactive. Without scheduling, we will falter at the proactive; without flexibility, we'll be unavailable for the reactive.

For Those Who've Wasted It

But even when we aim intentionally to let love drive our schedules, none of us will execute perfectly, or even adequately. Sinners are chronic time-wasters and regularly fall prey to bouts of lovelessness. Even the most disciplined time-managers are vulnerable to substantive missteps every day.

So what do we do with regret over all the time we've squandered? God holds out this hope as we learn to love by managing our time: Redeem your wasted days, weeks, and years by letting them drive you to Jesus, and inspire you, by faith, to more carefully count the days still ahead.

When the gospel floods our soul, and our schedules, and we know deeply that "Christ Jesus has made me his own," then, in all our imperfections and indiscretions—but alive in faith, powered by the Spirit, and driven by love—we're able to "press on to make it my own" and "forgetting what lies behind and straining forward to what lies ahead . . . press on toward the goal for the prize of the upward call of God in Christ Jesus" (Phil. 3:12–14).

You may always be on the clock, but the mercies of Christ are new every morning. Even every hour.

Four Lessons in Fruitful Time Management

Finally, to the tune of making some of these principles more specific and practical, here are four lessons in fruitful time management, for the mission of love.

1. CONSIDER YOUR CALLING

God has gifted each of us for the common good (1 Cor. 12:7). He empowers a variety of gifts, services, and activities among his people (12:4–6). In terms of our professional "calling," often we find it easier to identify what it is God might be moving us toward in the future, rather than what he has presently called us to today. For instance, it can be difficult for the business student, sensing a "call" to one day do business for the glory of God, to realize that his present calling is that of a student, even as he moves toward his perceived future call in business.

Our professional calling—that regular endeavor for which God has designed our head, heart, and hands for some particular season of life—flows not only from our own aspirations and the affirmations of others, but also from a tangible opportunity.

One of us might feel the call to some new profession, and have the happy approval of those who know us best, but until some specific door swings open and we have the live opportunity to begin operating in that field, that calling remains future—and we neglect our previous charge to the detriment of our joy and the good of others.

2. PLAN WITH BIG STONES

Next, in light of God's calling on us today, identify the key priorities that make up that calling. Typically, these priorities will be considerably compromised, if not abandoned altogether, if we don't plan for them with some intentionality.

Some have called these "the big stones."[4] The little pebbles are the smaller things to which we regularly give time but don't contribute directly to the main priorities of our calling. If we put the big stones first into the jar of our schedule, we'll be able to fill the cracks with a good many pebbles. But if we put the pebbles in first, the big stones likely will not fit.

3. MAKE THE MOST OF YOUR MORNINGS

Learn a lesson from the psalmists (Pss. 5:3; 30:5; 46:5; 59:16; 88:13; 90:5–6, 14; 92:2; 143:8), and from Jesus himself (Mark 1:35), and from many of the "greats" in the church's history, and make the most of your mornings.

Study after study confirms the importance of the first hours of the day for fulfilling the most important (and often most intensive) aspects of our calling. In the morning, we're typically our sharpest and have the largest store of energy to work creatively and proactively. Also, in the morning we're less likely to be sidelined by interruptions and the urgencies that arise as the day wears on.

---

[4] Ibid., 197.

How we regularly invest our mornings can be telling. How many of us have found it true that where our morning is, there our heart will be also? When our top priority each day is re-orienting toward Jesus and hearing his voice in the Scriptures, we'll be more likely to create space for that early, and less likely to leave it to chance that something won't drown it out later in the day.

Then, vocationally, how we spend those first few hours on the clock can be critical. As difficult as it can be to resist pro-crastinating on our most intensive and demanding tasks ("the big stones"), the most strategic time to tackle them is first thing in the morning. As to how guarding our mornings like this might be driven by love, think of it this way: In defending the light of our early mornings from trifles, we free ourselves to go on the offensive to beat back the darkness with flexibility for unscheduled acts of love later in the day. This leads to a fourth and final lesson.

4. Create Flexibility for Meeting Others' Needs

So far, we've been mostly implicit about how these broad time management lessons function in the service of love. Now let's get explicit.

On the one hand, our careful consideration of calling, and planning in light of key priorities, and making the most of the day's first hours all function in the service of love as the proac-tive output of our vocation to serve and bless others. This is, after all, what our calling is in its truest and deepest sense: how God has prepared for us, with our particular abilities, in a cer-tain season of life, to regularly expend time and energy for the good of others. That's the proactive dimension to our calling.

But on the other hand, knowing our giftings and attend-ing to our priorities and tackling them first thing in the morn-ing also unleashes us to be reactive as the day unfolds, able to respond to the unplanned needs of others, whether big or small, obvious or subtle. Love both plans for fixed blocks to push forward our proactive labors of love as well as allows margin and flexibility to attend to others' unplanned needs as they arise.

Remember Jesus's Words

It's a Christian Hedonistic way to parcel your time. It's a way for us to remember the words of Jesus, how he himself said, "It is more blessed to give than to receive" (Acts 20:35). The greatest joys come not from time squandered, hoarded, or selfishly spent, but from self-sacrificial love for others to the glory of God, when we pour out our time and energy for the good of others, and find our joy in theirs.

After all, acts of love don't just happen.

Communing with Christ on a Crazy Day

———

We've all been there. Maybe even today is one of those days for you. The crazy day. At least spiritually speaking.

Hopefully you are developing your regular routine and go-to "habits of grace," your own *when* and *where* and *how*s for seeking daily communion with God. Perhaps you've been at this long enough that when the alarm goes off *on a normal day*, you have your emerging patterns and rhythms for how getting up and getting breakfast and getting ready all come together in relation to some short but substantive season of "getting in the Word," to reset your mind and refill your heart and recalibrate your perspective before diving into the day.

But then comes those crazy days. And they seem to pop up more frequently than we're expecting. It may be the late-night conversation, important but tiring, that has you hitting the snooze over and over the next morning. Or maybe it's staying over with relatives, or having them squatting at your place.

Or for young parents, it's the child (or the children) who was up during the night, or rolled out of bed way too early wanting breakfast and your attention. Or maybe it's just this season of life, and honestly every morning seems to have its own craziness. The Enemy seems to have some new, creative scheme with each new day to keep you from finding any focused "time alone with God."

Whatever the circumstances that throw a wrench into your routine, your crazy mornings raise the question, How should you think about, and engage in (if at all), the means of grace of Bible meditation and prayer when God's good, but often inconvenient, sovereignty has you reeling without your routine?

1. Remember What Your "Habits of Grace" Are About

A good place to begin is with the big picture about your morning spiritual routines. Bible meditation is not about checking boxes, but communion with the risen Christ in and through his word. Walking in his grace today is not dependent on you going through your full devotional routine, or any routine for that matter. It is the regular pattern of communion with Christ that is vital, not extended time on one particular day.

You could read all the passages, give time to extensive journaling in meditation and prayer, work at length on memorizing Scripture, and easily move right into a day of walking in your own strength and not dying to selfish interests to anticipate and act to meet the needs of others. In fact, it is likely the days when you feel strongest personally, and most spiritually accomplished, that you're most prone to walk in your own strength, rather than by the strength that God supplies (1 Pet. 4:11).

2. Consider the Path of Love

It is loving (to others) to regularly commune with God. There are good horizontal effects to having our souls established and flourishing vertically. You will be a better spouse and parent and friend and cousin and child and neighbor if your soul is being routinely shaped and sustained by a real relationship with God in his word and prayer.

Sometimes, the most loving thing we can do is get away from people for a few minutes, feed our souls on God and his goodness, and come back to our families and communities reenergized for anticipating and meeting others' needs. But at other times, the path of love is dying to our desires for personal time alone—even in such good things as Bible meditation and prayer—to give attention to the toddler who is sick or woke up early, or to prepare and serve breakfast to family from out of town, or to assist a spouse or friend who is having his own crazy morning.

3. Develop a Morning Routine That Is Adaptable

Taking the crazy mornings into account, knowing that they will come and trying to be ready for them, may mean that you develop morning habits that are flexible. Try to create a routine that can expand into more than an hour if you have it, or collapse into just ten minutes, or even less, when love requires it.

For example, you might consider a simple pattern like the one we've been moving toward in this book: *Begin with Bible reading, move into meditation, polish with prayer.* On days when you have extended time, you can read and meditate longer, and include journaling, and take time to put some rich passage to memory, and linger in prayer, from adoration to confession to thanksgiving to supplication. But on a crazy morning, you can get through the reading-meditation-prayer sequence in just a few brief minutes if needed.

Instead of reading all the assigned passages in your Bible-reading plan, just take one short psalm or little Gospel account or small section of an epistle. Look for one manifestation of

God's goodness in the passage, and meditate on that goodness being for you in Jesus and try to press the truth into your heart. Then pray that truth in light of your day and the needs at hand, along with any other spontaneous requests on your mind that morning.

If time is really tight, at least pause briefly to pray, and seek to carry a spirit of prayer and dependence into the day. Christ can meet you on the move. Express to God that it seems circumstances and the call of love are leading you right into life today. Acknowledge that you can't earn his help with a long season of meditation and prayer, and ask that he would show himself strong today by being your strength when you feel spiritually weak.

Actually, it's often the crazy days when we feel most dependent, and our sense of weakness is good for God showing us his strength. "My grace is sufficient for you, for my power is made perfect in weakness" (2 Cor. 12:9).

4. Look for God's Provision through Others

The means of grace aren't simply personal. They are profoundly corporate. Even our personal Bible meditation and prayer are deeply shaped by our lives in community, and by those who have taught us intentionally. Personal Bible intake and prayer can be powerful—and they are habits of grace worth pursuing daily—but so can a reminder of God's grace from a spouse or friend or fellow believer. Don't neglect the power of fellowship as a means of God's grace.

If time alone with Jesus just isn't happening on this crazy morning, be on special lookout for some morsel of gospel food from conversation with someone who loves Jesus. If it's a crazy day for both of you, perhaps some quick conversation, pointing each other to Christ and his goodness toward us, would produce some food for you both that you otherwise wouldn't have had.

5. Evaluate Later What You Might Learn for Next Time

When the crazy morning and day has passed, seek to learn how you can grow in anticipating and tackling these in the future. If you stayed up too late to watch some show or movie needlessly, the lesson may be, very simply, to plan ahead better next time. Though often there's nothing to learn. This is just life in this age.

The crazy days will come. And there are seasons of life, like with a newborn at home, where all bets are off and it's just a crazy season. But with a little intentionality, and with a modest plan in place, you can learn to navigate these days, and even walk with greater dependence on God, knowing full well that it's not the ideal execution of our morning habits of grace that secures his favor and blessing.

You can commune with Christ in the crazy days.

Thanks

———

It takes a village—to raise a child and to write a book. My journey with the habits of grace goes back to childhood, even before I can remember. Mom and Pop not only sought to cultivate their own communion with Jesus in daily Bible reading and prayer, but they made the habit of gathering us children for family devotions before bed. Under Christ himself, my first expression of thanks is for Mom and Pop.

Next comes the patient and kind middle school and high school parent-volunteers at First Baptist Church in Spartanburg, South Carolina. Too many to name invested in us on countless Sunday mornings and evenings and Wednesday nights. Beyond the youth leaders, it was pastor Don Wilton who taught us that we could trust the Bible, and Seth Buckley who was the paragon of both youth ministry and Christian manhood.

In college at Furman University in Greenville, South Carolina, the seminal influences were disciplers Faamata Fonoimoana and Matt Lorish, under the leadership of Ken Currie. Faamata sacrificed of himself as an upperclassman to invest in lowly freshmen. He was a disciplemaker in all of life, habits of grace included. Then after two years with Faamata, Matt took me under his wing my last two years at Furman. He assigned Donald S. Whitney's *Spiritual Disciplines for the Christian Life* and trusted me enough to teach younger students publicly at summer training projects.

Now in these twelve years in Minnesota, the influences have multiplied. Paul Poteat, Matt Reagan, and Andrew Knight lived together with me this vision of daily communion with Jesus, as we discipled it into college students.

Special thanks goes to my former coworker and now fellow pastor, Jonathan Parnell, who sent the fateful, unsolicited email on December 28, 2011: "I wonder if you should consider writing a book on the disciplines. . . . Think about it." Well, I did. And even though it seemed like a long shot at first, the opportunity came to teach the disciplines to collegiates at Bethlehem College & Seminary (BCS), and then write about them at desiringGod.org. Finally Crossway was kind to provide the space and support to grow the seedlings into the book you hold in your hands. Thanks in particular to Ryan Griffith at BCS, content-team colleagues at desiringGod.org (Marshall Segal, Tony Reinke, Phillip Holmes, Stefan Green, John Piper, and Jon Bloom), and the dear friends at Crossway, especially Justin Taylor, who believed in this project enough to suggest we make a study guide. Thanks to all-star editor Tara Davis for tackling this project with such expertise and care, and to Pam Eason for her help and direction on the study guide.

Thank you to my wife, Megan, twin sons Carson and Coleman, and new daughter Gloria. You made adjustments to give me the time to sew the final threads together in January and August of 2015. And Megan, for more than eight years now, you have been my happy partner in cultivating habits of grace and making our home a matrix for hearing God's voice, having his ear, and belonging to his body. This book would not exist without your encouragement, patience, and remarkable grace.

Finally, and most importantly, to the God-man, seated in power on the throne of the universe, under whose wise and kind sovereignty the seeds for this little book were planted and nourished in the soil and water of his merciful providence. Indeed, the lines have fallen for me in pleasant places (Ps. 16:6). My prayer is that Jesus—Lord, Savior, and greatest treasure— may be more duly loved and cherished and enjoyed through this little book. May it inspire many habits of his grace in his admirers, in light of his glorious means of grace in his word, ear, and body. And may the great end truly be that he is all the more our great treasure (Matt. 13:44) and exceeding joy (Ps. 43:4).

General Index

Scripture Index

desiringGod

Everyone wants to be happy. Our website was born and built for happiness. We want people everywhere to understand and embrace the truth that *God is most glorified in us when we are most satisfied in him.* We've collected more than thirty years of John Piper's speaking and writing, including translations into more than forty languages. We also provide a daily stream of new written, audio, and video resources to help you find truth, purpose, and satisfaction that never end. And it's all available free of charge, thanks to the generosity of people who've been blessed by the ministry.

If you want more resources for true happiness, or if you want to learn more about our work at Desiring God, we invite you to visit us at www.desiringGod.org.

www.desiringGod.org

Deepen Your Understanding of *Habits of Grace* with the Study Guide

Developed for both individual and small group use, this companion to *Habits of Grace* features key Scripture readings, practical reflection questions, and prompts for prayer—equipping you to keep the gospel at the center as you develop habits that put you in the path of God's grace.

Available Now